First Aid

for the

Spirit

A MESSAGE FOR SPIRITUAL HEALING, THAT WILL HELP STRENGTHEN THE FOUNDATION OF YOUR FAITH - By David A. Rose, Sr.

"And by His stripes we are healed." (Isaiah 53:5)

ISBN 978-1-64416-155-5 (paperback)
ISBN 978-1-64416-156-2 (digital)

Christian Faith Publishing, Inc.
832 Park Avenue
Meadville, PA 16335
www.christianfaithpublishing.com

Printed in the United States of America

CONTENTS

FOREWORD

I am humbled to be blessed with the opportunity to write a fore-
word for this spirit led masterpiece, "First Aid for The Spirit",
written by my dear Cousin, David Rose.

It was a wakeup call to my spirit as I critiqued this God led
endeavor. I was particularly impressed with the prayers at the end
of each chapter which gives the reader an opportunity to close some
doors that have been opened to Satan during their life.

If persons who read this book do so with an open mind, spirit
and heart, it will cause wonderful changes in their lives.

These writings are truly "First Aid for The Spirit". We all need
to realize we've sinned and fallen short along our pathway of life, but
we serve a mighty awesome God who loves us and gladly gives us
another chance at living in His way and will.

"To God Be the Glory", David, "for the great things He's done".
I know our family members, who are no longer with us, would be
very proud of the godly man you've become. Continue to listen and
obey His voice.

Harrilene Beane Simmons Shackelford,
Superannuated Elder of the African Methodist Episcopal Church
January 08, 2018

David and I grew up in a family of five, two brothers and one
sister. David is about six years older than me and our sister, Renee, is
about two years older than David. Needless to say, David and Renee
were quite close due to their proximity in age, but David and I always
had a special bond since we were brothers. Our parents were God

fearing people that always wanted each of us to have a better life than they did. Even though Mom and Dad never completed college, they managed to successfully put all three of us through college.

Over the years David and I have endured some hardships and pain. Mom passed away in November of 1985 at the early age of fifty-five from a bout with cancer, Dad passed away suddenly in July of 2002 at the age of 72, and Renee died from cancer in September of 2013 at the age of 59. Having suffered through each of these losses, David and I thankfully have grown closer to God rather than away from him. I do believe that our trials have made us stronger and allowed us to gain a better relationship with God. So what was supposed to bring us down actually served to build us up and help us to clarify what God has in store for our lives.

"First Aid for the Spirit" is the fruit of that revelation and is an inspiring work for anyone desiring a closer walk with God.

Walter C. Rose
Frederick, Maryland
Brother of the author
January 8, 2018

The writer of this book has tremendous theological insight to the importance of establishing an absorption and fulfillment of God's Holy Word. He makes it clear that the years in family church, didn't give him the spiritual satisfaction until he was submersed and fulfilled with God's anointing and understanding of his Holy Word.

The book covers many areas that impact upon our social, political, and spiritual development as we prepare to enter into the present kingdom of God. Many have refused to explore this area but the true word must be understood and studied as the author emphasizes.

The reason we have lost so many of our youth today is because the word has not been clearly taught and shared by those who profess to be our spiritual leaders.

The author provides spiritual examples that certainly lead to wholly rely upon the word of God.

There is also great emphasis on faith and trust in almighty God. "Thou shalt love the Lord thy God with all thy heart, and with all thy soul" (Matthew 22:37)

This is God's first and greatest commandment, and then we should love our neighbor as ourselves.

The reader will truly experience an unrelenting love for Christ who gave His life for us, but this can only happen with a true comprehension of the word.

I challenge you to read the book and it will cause you to inhale so much knowledge that you will become very anxious to exhale, sharing joy to a sinful world.

Rev. Louis D. Sanders (retired 2017)
Senior Pastor: St. Charles A.M.E. Zion Church, Sparkill, NY
March 12, 2018

INTRODUCTION

Hope is the vision of that which exists just beyond the horizon. This hope is what we need to sustain our day-to-day living. Without it, our vision of the future would change from the glory of a sunrise to a rapidly darkening sunset, or a future of promise to a life of seemly inescapable defeat. Everyone needs hope to survive.

> *Now faith is confidence in what we hope for and*
> *assurance about what we do not see. (Hebrews 11:1)*

Whenever you rely only on physical vision for the fulfillment of future dreams, the world can create a false picture that is sometimes very difficult to overcome. On the other hand, a spiritually minded person walks through life by faith and not by physical sight. By moving into this level of belief in God, it will not matter what picture the world paints before us. Our eyes are not the key to vision but, rather, our heart that has been transformed by God. True vision is based on the appropriate level of faith, ever increasing with one's knowledge of God's word and not by what is seen with the naked eye.

This book was conceived with God's guidance and direction to offer insight into answering basic spiritual questions and to help Christian believers heal spiritually from the pain and suffering encountered in daily living. We are spiritual beings housed in a physical body. Whether it is placing a Band-Aid on a small cut or scrape, stitching an open wound, mending a broken limb, or administering medicine to control an allergic reaction, this physical shell will require many forms of first aid in a lifetime. Because of our sins, our spirits will also fall prey to all types of injuries, which to will leave us hurt, wounded, scared, and broken.

To survive, spiritual first aid is available to treat the wounds inflicted by the world. It will mend broken hearts, heal fractured relationships, close the wounds of hatred and indifference, and rescue souls drowning in despair. This first aid does not start on the outside of the physical body, but rather on the inside of the spirit. It starts with faith in Jesus Christ and his healing grace. Through Jesus Christ, no pain is impossible or sorrow too great to bear.

Jesus Christ suffered and died for our sins, so that we would not have to experience spiritual death. The word of God is our guide to living in such a way as to prevent spiritual injury and death. Let's live the life that God has destined for us. But if we stumble and fall, we will know that by faith, our First Aid is only a prayer away.

> *But he was pierced for our transgressions, he was crushed for our iniquities; the punishment that brought us peace was on him, and by his wounds we are healed. (Isaiah 53:5)*

WORDS OF THANKS

First, I would like to thank God for using me for this project and I hope that it will educate and enlighten others to his infinite grace and mercy as well as the knowledge, wisdom and understanding he has given us through his holy word. It was a great honor to put this book together and to be one of his obedient servants for the kingdom.

To my beautiful wife Vicki, that God sent to be my sole-mate for over thirty-six years. You have truly been the one who, with the help of God, kept me spiritually grounded in the Lord. You have been strong when I was weak and wise when my judgment became impaired. You are my true friend for life.

To my parents Calvin and Eleanor, who left this life sooner than I would have liked, but God is in control. You taught me to be a good and honest person and to carry myself with pride, dignity and honor, while always putting God first in everything that I undertake. I truly miss your presence, but always feel your spirit is with me.

To my big sister Renee, who passed in 2013, for the wonderful trips and talks we had together and how you encouraged me at the start of this project with positive words of motivation to keep going. I truly miss her beautiful smile and calm spirit.

To my younger brother Walter, who is wise beyond his years, I thank you for always having the right words to say when I need them. Although, distance may keep us apart physically, God has always bonded us spiritually. We have so much in common with our families, hobbies and our faith, and that we let God use us for his service. May God continue to bless you and your family.

To all my wonderful children, Tiffani, David ll, Daniel and Tia, I thank you for making me so proud with all the godly service you are doing in your individual communities. I see how all of you are always willing to serve in your church, community and schools, while still taking time to help others in need. The bible says you are known by the fruit that you bear and the four of you always make my tree look full of good fruit. I will love you always.

To my support team: Uncle Archie and Barbara Richmond, Al and Earline Thomas, Robert and Sandy Holman, Gil and Sybille Noble and Aunt Laurie Peery, who have prayed and supported me in everything that I have ever done. They have also been a blessing to my wife and children in so many ways over the years. My life would not be the same without your kindness and love. I will forever be indebted to you all.

To Rev. Harrilene Shackelford, Deacon Walter Rose and Rev. Louis Sanders for all of their wonderful words of encouragement, stated in their forewords. You are true children of God and I will always be indebted to you for your praise and spiritual perception concerning this project.

To all of my family members, pastors, teachers and friends who have supported me over the years, I would like you to know how much our relationship means to me. If not for your love and support, I would not be able to complete a project such as this. All of you have been my "First aid for the Spirit"

PURPOSE

F irst aid: The emergency treatment administered to injured or sick persons before professional medical care is available.

In 2000, my family and I were searching for a new church home in Memphis, Tennessee. The church we attended previously changed leadership, which resulted in a physical and spiritual division among the fellowship. As a result of the pastoral transition, along with the conflicting congregational issues, we decided to join World Overcomers Outreach Ministries Church (WOOMC), under the leadership of Apostle Alton R. Williams.

Apostle Williams is a wonderful pastor and shepherd. He believes in educating his members on the word of God and how it relates to us on a daily basis. He truly believes that the more spiritual knowledge, wisdom, and understanding we have inside our hearts and minds, the more equipped we will be to operate within the world's system without conforming to its way of life.

Shortly, after becoming members of the WOOMC family, my wife and I were required to complete a thirteen-week "Perfecting Class" program. The classes were designed to provide us with the necessary spiritual foundation needed for spiritual growth and fulfilling the positional duties in any of the many help ministries that we may wish to join. In keeping with the vision of our pastor, this allowed us to grow stronger in our faith and giving us a deeper understanding into the word of God.

My wife went on to play an important role in several youth ministry projects, in the area of drama, dance, and music within the children's ministries. My job with the airline kept me out of town, so I never joined any of the help ministries. However, as a result of the "perfecting classes," I soon realized that God had given me a personal help mission, which was the inspiration to write this book *First Aid for the Spirit.*

While attending these classes, the information I received helped me realize just how powerful we can be through God's word. I started to share some of this new-found wisdom with my fellow coworkers and soon realized that they were just as blind as I had been to the wisdom and power that God has given us to overcome the problems that we face daily. God provided me with these words that will hopefully help you perfect your faith and provide some well-needed first aid for a broken spiritual life.

Since the day I was born, my family and I attended church every Sunday. It was a small family church, Bethel African Methodist Episcopal Church, in Roanoke, Virginia, which was founded in 1867 by four Christian men, one being my great, great grandfather Mr. Bowyer Beane, who was a Native American from the Cherokee tribe. This church is still there and is recognized as a local historical landmark.

While attending Bethel AME, I accepted Jesus Christ as my Lord and savior in my early teens and was baptized. When I went off to college, I may have attended church twice in the four-and-a-half years of study, but always attended when I went home on the weekend or during school breaks. I am mentioning this because as a result of the information I gained from the WOOMC's "perfecting classes," I soon realized that although I had gone to church all my life and was saved by the blood of Jesus Christ, spiritually I was still very immature in my faith. I had a very weak spiritual immune system, but thanks to God's divine mercy and infinite grace, along with the prayers of my family, I survived. I came from a strong praying family, which paid the premium on my grace and mercy policy that I let lapse many times.

The main purpose of this book is to help us become aware of the power that we have spiritually, and that will inevitably help us achieve a higher quality of life physically. Also, by studying God's word, we can do battle with the enemy without self-doubt, worry, and fear. It all boils down to becoming a more mature Christian and an effective member of the body of Christ.

As the name of WOOMC proclaims, we are all world overcomers, and it is time that we started acting the part. We have to stop letting the world dictate our future, but rather allow God to define our destiny. It is my prayer and hope that this book can be used as the foundation upon which we can rebuild our faith in God and his Son Jesus Christ as well as discovering the blueprint of God's will for our life.

In 2001, I took a voluntary leave of absence from my job with the airline to pursue my dream of being a general contractor and building homes like my brother-in-law, Robert Holman, in Georgia. My first project was on a very large, uneven lot, which would require a very detailed foundation layout. It tested my limited knowledge and fresh contractor skills, but the job was successfully completed as planned. It was then that I realized that like this beautiful home, nothing will remain standing without a strong, well-designed foundation. This book was conceived to help build the foundation of our faith to a degree that the daily trials and tribulations will not cause us to fall. This book can be the first aid we need to heal from the wounds of life's trials that are certain to come.

> Therefore everyone who hears these words of mine
> and puts them into practice is like a wise man who
> built his house on the rock. (Matthew 7:24)

The next time we become afflicted by daily trials and tribulations, we should petition God for the healing we need. The Bible is our *first-aid* manual, and prayer is our 911 call to our heavenly Father. As we mature in our faith, we will soon realize healing is only a prayer away. So, in our hour of brokenness, remember what the word of God said in the book of *1 Peter 2:24, "He himself bore our sins" in his body on the cross, so that we might die to sins and live for righteousness; "by his wounds you have been healed."*

During the course of our lives, there will be times that some degree of *first aid* will be required. It does not matter whether it is for a major accident or minor illness, the need will eventually arise. The longer we live, the more we will realize that things happen that are totally out of our control. Since we cannot control or predict the future, we need to find something to help us believe that no matter what the future brings, we have faith in the fact that there will always be someone there by our side to help us see it through. God is the one who will always answer our emergency call for help, and only our faith in Him will enable us to receive the care that we need to heal and become whole again.

Once we discover that we are both physical and spiritual beings, we will realize that some degree of *first aid* will be required to treat these injuries, which will occur in both of these areas in our lives. This book is meant to be a source of information about the healing powers that have been woven into the gospel for us to use as spiritual medicine, which will protect and relieve us from the cuts and bruises that we will encounter along the way.

Since we are born with a sinful nature that drives our desire to satisfy the flesh, we will always be yielding to worldly temptations of one kind or the other. It is for this reason that we suffer wounds as the consequence of our sin.

> *We know that the law is spiritual; but I am unspiritual, sold as a slave to sin. 15 I do not understand what I do. For what I want to do I do not do, but what I hate I do. (Romans 7:14–15)*

God knew that the independent nature of man would always have him warring with the flesh to sin. When his son Jesus left us physically, he sent us a comforter called the Holy Spirit to be with us at all times and be the spiritual voice of reason, which resides in the heart and guides us to do that which is within the will of God. Once we learn to become more sensitive to this godly inner voice, we may not suffer less, however, we will recover from the problems that are sure to arise.

> *For the wages of sin is death, but the gift of God is eternal life in[a] Christ Jesus our Lord. (Romans 6:23)*

Sin, in most instances, does not lead to physical death. However, sin without repentance will ultimately result in spiritual death, which is eternal damnation, the exact opposite of God's gift of eternal life. This is the reason we are going to need spiritual first aid during our lives, to repair the damage incurred by way of our sinful actions.

The God-given purpose for this book on spiritual *first aid* is to help us understand our true nature and why we find it so easy to sin while, at the same time, struggle to do that which is good and righteous. We will cover the origin of sin by our ancestors, Adam and Eve, along with their first sin of disobedience to God. This led to man's downfall and death by the flood. God's son Noah kept his word alive until the days of Moses, who brought us the Ten Commandments as a guide to keep us in compliance with his holy will. Once we received these rules for which we are to live by, God sent Jesus Christ, our Lord and savior. He taught us how to use our faith in order to live within these rules in the physical and spiritual realm.

> *You belong to your father, the devil, and you want to carry out your father's desires. He was a murderer from the beginning, not holding to the truth, for there is no truth in him. When he lies, he speaks his native language, for he is a liar and the father of lies. (John 8:44)*

Satan is the ruler of all earthly things, because that's the position given to him by God after he was cast out from heaven. Man was formed from the clay of the earth, and this connection is why Satan has such a strong influence over our flesh. This is how he communicates with our spirit, and since he is the author of confusion and the father of lies, we think the inner voice that we are hearing is God's, so we become spiritually confused and fall into the trap of sin. This is why we must develop an intimate relationship with God, so we will know his word and the voice of the Holy Spirit when they are speaking to us. This type of relationship with God, Jesus, and the Holy Spirit is all the first aid our spirit will ever need to help us live a healthier spiritual life.

Remember: Some politician's lie to win, taxpayers cheat on returns, married couples have affairs, people discriminate and hate others who are different, and sexual perversion is on the rise on every social level. The result of these acts of sin are like spiritual cancer to the guilty individual. Suffering from the sickness of sin and disobedience will become terminal and cause a slow spiritual death if left untreated. We do these things because we do not fear God and because we don't know him or possess his heart. But there is a way of healing for us with God's First aid for the Spirit.

CHAPTER ONE

In the Beginning
The Birth of Sin

The Birth

"In the beginning God created the heavens and the earth. Now the earth was formless and empty, darkness was over the surface of the deep, and the Spirit of God was hovering over the waters. And God said, "Let there be light," and there was light. As stated in the book of Genesis 1:1–3, this is where all forms of life began, and by faith, we hold these facts of God's wonderful creation to be true.

> Now faith is confidence in what we hope for and assurance about what we do not see. (**Hebrews 11:1**)
> And without faith it is impossible to please God, because anyone who comes to him must believe that he exists and that he rewards those who earnestly seek him. (Hebrews 11:6)

God created the world in six days. Some theological scholars may believe that a day to God is more than a thousand years by our worldly means of measurement. The point is not how long it actually took him to complete this marvelous work but rather how much faith one needs to truly believe it to be his creation. So, we can conclude that, by faith, we know it's real and with this same belief, we will please him. He created everything out of nothing, formed light from total darkness, and made all living things that exist. Then, he made his greatest creation, Man.

Once the earth and its inhabitants were created, God decided to create man to serve and worship him. Man was also given dominion over all the earth and living things. God knew he needed someone to manage the earth physically while he guided man spiritually. All living things that God created were made with a skillfully designed purpose to fill in this new world system, and they performed it perfectly without going against the creator's authority. Man, on the other hand, was given free will, which allowed him to go against God's wishes if he chose to do so. The only thing that would keep man in line with God's rules and regulations was the spirit of obedience, which connects him directly to God.

> Then God said, "Let us make mankind in our image,
> in our likeness, so that they may rule over the fish in
> the sea and the birds in the sky, over the livestock and
> all the wild animals,[a] and over all the creatures
> that move along the ground." (Genesis 1:26)

God stated, "Let *us* make mankind in *our* image." The fact that he said "us" addresses the presence of more than one entity. The "us" in this case is the Holy Trinity representing God the father, Jesus the son, and the Holy Spirit, our comforter, who are one and the same. Further proof of this is found in the book of John 1:1.

> In the beginning was the Word, and the Word was
> with God, and the Word was God. (John 1:1)

God states that man was created in *our* image. Again, he makes a reference to the fact that man was made in the spiritual image of himself, Jesus Christ, and the Holy Spirit. This spiritual life force was what God blew into man to give him physical life. Since man was formed from the clay of the earth, he was born with an inherited sinful nature, because Satan has dominion over all earthly things. He was given this authority to rule all earthly things by God when he was cast out of heaven for being disobedient. Satan, who was the archangel Lucifer, along with a host of angels who followed him, were cast out of heaven because he thought he was the true son of God.

Men and women were created for the sole purpose of serving God with their obedience to his laws and serving in his kingdom. They were to tend to the garden, manage all the animals and creatures, and be fruitful and multiply the earth with their seed. God knew that Adam and Eve would teach their children to serve him, and he also realized their children would also go astray, just as they had done.

The reason we are here is to serve God and make the world a better place, in which we all can live. We are the hands, eyes, ears, feet and voice of God. He uses us to get things done on the earth. This is why we must develop a closer relationship with him, so we can understand our divine purpose for being here. We are all pieces in the jigsaw puzzle of life, and the picture can never be completed if we come up missing. We are missing when we live in disobedience to his word and being disobedient comes with consequences.

The Death

Man was given a heavenly place to live, called the Garden of Eden. The Garden of Eden was pure heaven, with no pain, no suffering, no worries, and, for a while, no sin. Adam and Eve had only one rule to obey, which I will refer to as the first commandment. This rule was not to eat from the tree of the knowledge of good and evil. God told them that if they did, they would surely die. The resulting death for breaking this law, the law of disobedience, was not meant to mean instant physical death but rather spiritual death. This spiritual death would soon trigger other events that would lead man on the path to physical death. This ended man's gift of eternal life.

We are now on an individual quest to get this gift back by our belief in Jesus Christ, righteous living, and obedience to his law.

> *For the wages of sin is death; but the gift of God is*
> *eternal life in Jesus Christ our Lord. (Romans 6:23)*

The inherited sinful nature of man from Adam and Eve's sin caused this curse to be with us and all the generations that are to come. It is for this reason that our desire to sin is easier and seemingly more enjoyable than those things which are of a godly nature. Since we possess this inherited nature to sin, it will always come into conflict with our Godly spiritual side.

> *We know that the law is spiritual; but I am unspir-*
> *itual, sold as a slave to sin. (Romans 7:14)*

The words by one of Jesus' greatest disciples, Apostle Paul, tells us that we are one being under the influence of two different spiritual laws. The two separate natures of man are at war with each other daily, trying to control our soul. We are a spirit, with a soul, that lives in a physical body. Whoever controls the soul will control the whole being. This battle will be very difficult for a person who is spiritually weak in their faith in God and ignorant of his law.

God created men and women with the ability to make their own decisions by giving them free will. All other creatures are controlled by a natural order. This natural order has been called the laws of nature and establishes a pattern considered to be the circle of life. God knew that the independent nature of man, which is driven by his worldly desires, had to be conquered before he could get the gift back. This is why he sent his son Jesus, the word and the light, wrapped in human flesh and conceived through immaculate conception, by way of a virgin mother, to save us from our own sinful nature. Jesus was sent to overcome the temptations of the flesh by living a sin-free life. He conquered death through the resurrection and, in the process, became the blood atonement for our sins.

In order to stay spiritually healthy, we really need to know just how God wants us to live. He wants us to feed on his word, so it will become a part of our spirit, which will become a light in the midst of earthly darkness to others around us.

We will never be able to live a sin-free life, because our nature is to fulfill the desires of our flesh by way of sinful activities. We will experience pain and suffering as a result of it, but by the grace of God and his infinite mercy, he gave us a way to heal. This way is to love and obey him and to love our neighbors as ourselves. If we look back at all of the physical problems that we have experienced in our lives and relate them to God's word, we would quickly realize that most of them are the result of some act of disobedience to his law.

When we commit a sin, the hedge of protection that God has placed around us is slowly removed and is only restored when we become truly sorry and repent for our actions. Until this happens, the devil is free to inflict pain and suffering in our lives, but only within the limits that God will allow.

The Resurrection

Jesus was born without sin and lived without sinning but was crucified for our sins. God brought Jesus back to life with a new body so that he could live forever with him in heaven. He has the same plan for us, but we must first make the commitment to him, Jesus, and the Holy Spirit by being obedient to the law. Like Jesus Christ, our flesh must die to sinful ways to be born again spiritually.

If a healthier physical life is our desire, then we must first start with a healthier one spiritually. The spirit is built up by feeding on the bread of life, which is God's holy word. This is the only way that we can receive the power that we will need to fight off an enemy like Satan. If we continue to operate in this world, ignorant of God's law and disobedient to his will, then the wounds will never heal, and spiritually, we will bleed to death. Once the spirit dies, the body has no further reason to exist.

Obedience to God is the main challenge that Christians have to stay in good spiritual health. If physical longevity is a personal goal that we seek, then we must be willing to pay the price, which is the renewing of our mind to God's way of thinking. If we can do this, eternal life will be our final reward.

We can heal our spiritual wounds caused by life's darts and arrows by taking a daily dose of God's antibiotic, which is his holy word. By protecting ourselves with the armor that God has given us, we will avoid a lot of pain and suffering that is a result of sinful living. The armor of God that is described in his word is as follows:

> *Therefore put on the full armor of God, so that when the day of evil comes, you may be able to stand your ground, and after you have done everything, to stand.*
>
> *Stand firm then, with the belt of truth buckled around your waist, with the breastplate of righteousness in place, and with your feet fitted with the readiness that comes from the gospel of peace.*
>
> *In addition to all this, take up the shield of faith, with which you can extinguish all the flaming arrows of the evil one.*
>
> *Take the helmet of salvation and the sword of the Spirit, which is the word of God.*
>
> *And pray in the Spirit on all occasions with all kinds of prayers and requests. With this in mind, be alert and always keep on praying for all the Lord's people. (Ephesians 6:13–18)*

The following definitions will help explain the spiritual meaning of the various pieces of this godly armor.

1. *Loins girt with belt of truth:* Cover ourselves with the word of God, and through faith, it will protect our seed for future generations.

2. *Breastplate of righteousness:* The heavy metal used to protect the physical heart is the same as the mercy and grace that God sends us to protect our spiritual heart.

3. *Feet shod with the preparation of the gospel of peace:* The more we study the word of God, the more it will allow us to walk in his perfect peace. Then, he will order our steps.

4. *Shield of faith:* The strength of our faith in God will protect us from all manner of evil.

5. *Fiery darts of the wicked:* This represents the worldly temptations in life, sickness, addiction, financial problems, and ungodly attacks from others.

6. *Helmet of salvation:* Through our belief in the Holy Trinity, they will be able to protect our mind from the devil's control over our earthly desires, and they will always give us a means of escape from these temptations.

7. *Sword of the spirit:* The written and spoken word of God, like the sword, has two sides that will produce results at every point of contact.

8. *Prayer and supplication:* To ask or petition God for all of our needs.

Once we read the word and then receive true understanding of its spiritual content, then it can edify the spirit–man in us and allow God to protect our mind, body, and soul. He will rebuild the spiritual hedge around us that will aid us in our physical life as well.

Do not waste another day of pain and suffering trying to live by the world's rules. We must study his word to show ourselves approved, and God will order our steps and be the protector of our way. Always remember, God's *first aid* is only a prayer away.

A Prayer for Understanding

Lord, God, our most gracious heavenly father, we come to you with thanksgiving in our hearts for all the wonderful blessings that you have bestowed upon us. We know that you are aware of all our sinful ways and unrighteous acts against your law and others, of which we are truly sorry. We ask that you will forgive us and accept our spirit of true repentance for these transgressions. Endow us with your holy wisdom and the understanding to put it into action concerning every aspect of our lives. Anoint our minds with the righteous knowledge of your holy word so that we may be of service to you, oh, Lord. Help us to seek your will and walk in your way. In Jesus' holy name we pray. Amen.

Key Scriptures

Please read the entire chapter of each verse for greater edification and understanding.

1. Genesis 1: 1-3
2. Hebrews 11:1
3. Hebrews 11:6
4. Genesis 1:26
5. John 1:1
6. Romans 6:23
7. Romans 7:14–25
8. Ephesians 6:13–18

CHAPTER TWO

The Rules of the Game

For whoever keeps the whole law and yet stumbles at
just one point is guilty of breaking all of it. (James 2:10)

Are you ready for this journey called life? Life is like a game, because it requires certain rules that we must follow to survive while competing. There is a time, distance, weight, or score we must reach to achieve victory. Winning is usually associated with a trophy, medal, or prize money, as well as the feeling of great personal satisfaction. From the moment we were born, the game began, and our parents, relatives, friends, neighbors, teachers, and church members helped tech us the rules. As we grow older, our desire to compete becomes stronger, and our quest for victory gets more gratifying. However, the only way we are going to be truly victorious in this game is if we learn to play by God's rules.

They are not complicated, but they are without compromise. There is no gray area or shortcuts to this victory, and the reward is the same for everyone. The reward is eternal life through Jesus Christ. God used his servant Moses to deliver the rules to the people of Israel, and after the birth, death, and resurrection of Jesus Christ, everyone can now claim the prize. Only when we make an earnest attempt to follow these ten godly rules, will this reward be ours.

Along our daily walk, we must follow certain rules and regulations in order to operate in this worldly system. However, since we

DAVID A. ROSE, SR.

are both flesh and spirit, there are God's rules that we must follow as well. These rules or laws are very important for our spiritual relationship with him and how he will aid us in the physical phase of our journey.

I would like for you to take this Bible exercise, which is based on God's basic laws for everyone who confesses to be a born-again Christian. Below are ten blank spaces for you to write each of the Ten Commandments without the aid of your Bible. After you have completed this task, turn the page to review your answers and make a mental note of the ones missed.

1. _____
2. _____
3. _____
4. _____
5. _____
6. _____
7. _____
8. _____
9. _____
10. _____

Well, how did you fair concerning the rules that God has given us to live by every day? This exercise was used to enlighten you on the knowledge of his word as well as to make you aware that we cannot honor and obey laws that we do not remember or understand.

In my travels, I discovered that the majority of the people whom I have posed this question to could not name all ten either, so do not feel bad if you missed a few. These are God's rules of conduct for every human being who confesses to be saved and born again by the blood of his son Jesus Christ. So, how do we expect to obey God's laws if we do not know what they are? Our obedience to these laws are the key ingredients required by God to live a healthy spiritual life.

As we all know, a key is an instrument used to unlock a device so that we can gain excess to what's inside. These laws are the key that opens the door to God's blessings. Satan's plan is to keep us confused about God's laws, because if we do not remember them, then chances are we will disobey them without even being aware that we are doing anything wrong. Also, we are not going to repent from doing something that we feel is right, and thus the devil's plan is complete.

When we are driving, there are rules and regulations, traffic signs, lights, speed limits, and laws that we must obey. If we fail to obey the rules of the road and get caught, then we will have to pay the price for our acts of disobedience. This price can sometimes be very costly financially and may result in the loss of our driving privileges, jail time, serious injury, or even death.

What if there were no rules or regulations, traffic signs, or lights for us to follow, but the negative outcome and punishments were the same? It would not seem fair, would it? We ask ourselves, "Why are we getting punished for breaking laws we did not know existed?" This is the reason for the written examination that we all must pass in order to get the privilege to drive.

In this journey of life, God has given us rules and regulations to follow, but Satan has managed to remove them from our hearts and mind, causing us to travel unprotected. In other words, our spiritual insurance policy has expired with God.

> *You belong to your father, the devil, and you want to carry out your father's desires. He was a murderer from the beginning, not holding to the truth, for there is no truth in him. When he lies, he speaks his native language, for he is a liar and the father of lies. (John 8:44)*

In the Garden of Eden, the devil lied to Eve to get her to disobey God's first rule about eating the forbidden fruit from the tree of knowledge of good and evil. She then passed the lie on to Adam, who also acted in disobedience, and being considered as one flesh in the eyes of God, they were both punished for their sin. Since they both sinned and fell short of the grace of God, their place in paradise came to an abrupt end, and God cancelled their eternal-life policy.

Satan wants to keep us ignorant of God's laws and his holy word. Let's go back to the basics and learn the Ten Commandments by heart. This way, they will become a part of us spiritually and physically. It will make our journey in life much easier, by allowing us to grow spiritually by the grace of God and allow his blessings to continue to flow in our lives.

Reviewing these commandments will allow us to receive the total understanding of the rules that he has given us to follow. And in doing so, we will discover how our unmindful disobedience of his laws will affect our relationship with him.

What We Should Do!

> *I. Thou shalt love the Lord thy God with all thy heart, and with all thy mind, and with all thy soul (Matthew 22:37)*

This is God's first and greatest commandment, because he knew that if we can love him whom we have not seen, then we can love others that we see every day.

> *No one has seen God; but if we love one another, God lives in us and his love is made complete in us. (1 John 4:12)*

If we love God, then we will honor him by our service to others and his house. Once we accept God as our heavenly father and Jesus Christ as his only begotten son as well as our Lord and savior, then our soul belongs to him. It was bought with a price, which was the blood that was shed by Jesus on the cross during the crucifixion.

Since we are now God's property and he is our master, we are obligated to love, worship, and serve him with all our mind, heart, and soul. If we fail to fulfill this first commandment, then the whole master–servant relationship will be out of order and will weaken our ability to resist sinful activities.

If you love me, keep my commands. (John 14:15)

We must understand that total love for God is not an option for a Christian but something that is required. So, until we reach the level of faith that will allow us to love him totally and completely, then our faith will be weak and ineffective. Let us strengthen our faith daily with the word of God, and this will draw us into a closer relationship with him. He loves us so much that he wrapped his spirit in flesh, walked the earth as a man, and while enduring tremendous pain and suffering, he chose to die for our sins. We must return this love to the master with our service to his holy kingdom while we are on this earth.

> *Remember: "For God so loved the world that he gave his one and only Son, that whoever believes in him shall not perish but have eternal life" (John 3:16).*

> *II. Thou shalt love thy neighbor as thy self (Matthew 22:38)*

As I heard this scripture as a child, I thought that my neighbors were only the people who lived on my block. I was only thinking within the narrow limitations of a child, without godly wisdom to give me the full understanding of his word. Now, I know that everyone is my neighbor regardless of their race, creed, color, or religious beliefs.

> *If you really keep the royal law found in Scripture, "Love your neighbor as yourself," you are doing right. (James 2:8)*

To do right by God, we must love everybody, and this includes our enemies. This is the system that God has given us to operate within, and in order to please him, we must obey his law. The consequences of being disobedient to the law of brotherly love is the same as that of any other sinful act against God's word. If we fail to love anyone for any reason, then we are operating outside the will of the Father.

> *How good and pleasant it is when God's people live together in unity! (Psalms 133:1*

Sin is the devil's tool that he uses to keep our relationship with God weak and ineffective. Until we let go of our petty differences and prejudices, we will literally hate our way into hell.

> *Hatred stirs up conflict, but love covers over all wrongs. (Proverbs: 10:12)*

All of us need to take a long hard look in the mirror and really search our hearts and souls on this matter of brotherly love. Think about it: If God can love us with all our many faults, then we should be able to show the same degree of love for one another.

> *But he wanted to justify himself, so he asked Jesus, "And who is my neighbor?"*
>
> *In reply Jesus said: "A man was going down from Jerusalem to Jericho, when he was attacked by robbers. They stripped him of his clothes, beat him and went away, leaving him half dead.*
>
> *A priest happened to be going down the same road, and when he saw the man, he passed by on the other side.*
>
> *So too, a Levite, when he came to the place and saw him, passed by on the other side.*
>
> *But a Samaritan, as he traveled, came where the man was; and when he saw him, he took pity on him.*
>
> *He went to him and bandaged his wounds, pouring on oil and wine. Then he put the man on*

*his own donkey, brought him to an inn and took
care of him.*

*The next day he took out two denarii[a] and
gave them to the innkeeper. 'Look after him,' he
said, 'and when I return, I will reimburse you for
any extra expense you may have.'*

*"Which of these three do you think was a neigh-
bor to the man who fell into the hands of robbers?"*

*The expert in the law replied, "The one who
had mercy on him."*

*Jesus told him, "Go and do likewise." (Luke
10:29–37)*

Let us obey the word of God and be a Good Samaritan, and he
will bless us for being a blessing to our neighbor, especially in their
time of need.

*III. Thou shalt remember the Sabbath day and keep
it holy (Exodus 20:8)*

Growing up in Roanoke, Virginia, which carries the distinctive
title as the Star City of the South because of the majestic eighty-
eight and a half foot neon star which stands atop Mill Mountain,
I remember all of the stores, gas stations, and business being closed
on Sundays. This was out of reverence to God and made legal by a
state wide ordinance known as the Blue Law, which was put into law
during the late 1700's.

Many cities had this law for quite a while. We all enjoyed this
day of rest, for worship, and for spending time with our family and
friends, but greed in the business world eventually forced the law to
be eliminated. Man felt a need to extend their services to the public
seven days a week. The business community stated that this was done
to better serve our needs, but in reality, it was only serving as a way
to increase their bottom line. This action puts our country out of the
will of God, which will open the door to curse us as a nation for our
disobedience to his word.

Whether people used their free time on Sundays to worship the Lord was an individual choice, but at least, we were free to spend the day as we pleased. This is not the case today, because many of us are forced into working on Sundays, while others have had their jobs terminated for refusing to work on the Sabbath due to their religious beliefs.

Man's love for capital gain overshadowed his love for God and the respect for his holy day. Once man puts his love for money over his desire to praise and worship him, then he is truly operating out of His will.

> *For the love of money is a root of all kinds of evil. Some people, eager for money, have wandered from the faith and pierced themselves with many griefs. (1 Timothy 6: 10)*

A root is the formation of a foundation from a seed of which everything grows. If we love money, then we cannot love God as well. When we love and covet money and material possessions that we can acquire, then we are guilty of two sins. Once these two problems become rooted in our lives, our faith will become weak and ineffective. This opens the door for Satan to take control of our finances, which will cause us great sorrow due to the love we possess for our wealth.

If we were to examine all the evil things that have happened in the past and present, we would discover that most of it is rooted in or related to some financial situation. God's will is for all of his children to prosper, because that's what a loving father would desire for his children. Nevertheless, his hands are tied from blessing us if we are not living according to his holy will.

> *If they obey and serve him, they will spend the rest of their days in prosperity and their years in contentment. (Job 36:11)*

I realize that there are jobs, such as, foodservices, shipping, and transportation, of which I am personally employed, that require us to work on Sunday. Also, there are jobs in the field of medicine which require twenty-four-hour services. However, if we operate our own businesses or have the option to choose not to work on the Sabbath, then the heavenly father will reward us for our obedience.

One of the best illustrations to prove we do not need to work on Sunday is a successful fast-food company called Chick-fil-A. It started in 1946 as the Dwarf Grill, in Atlanta, Georgia, by founder and chairman, Mr. S. Truett Cathy, a born-again Christian who truly believes in keeping God's word and living within his holy will.

In 1947, the Dwarf Grill became the first in-mall restaurant under the new name of Chick-fil-A. Mr. Cathy wanted to ensure that every Chick-fil-A restaurant owner and their employees had the opportunity to attend church services as well as spend time with their family and friends on Sunday. It made perfect sense to him then, and it still makes sense to him now. Even though their restaurants are closed on Sundays, they still continue to prosper and achieve success in the fast-food industry. Despite only operating out of over 2,400 *restaurants, Chick-fil-A ranks very* high in terms of its total sales, while averaging 3.1 million per store in sales daily. The chain generated nearly $10.46 billion in revenue in 2018, making it the 3rd-largest *fast-food* chain in the US, according to QSR.

> *Then he said to them, "The Sabbath was made for man, not man for the Sabbath. (Mark 2:27)*

Think of it this way. If the Sabbath were a national holiday, what would we do on this day? Would we work or celebrate the occasion? It is for this reason that our heavenly father expects nothing less than for us to honor his weekly holiday that he made just for us.

> *IV. Honor thy father and thy mother that thy days may be long upon which the Lord thy God giveth thee (Exodus 20:12)*

In reviewing this law, we will discover that God has a blessing in store for those who honor their earthly parents. This gift is God's promise to us that if we show love, compassion and respect for our parents, regardless of how they treat or care for us, then he will bless our life with physical longevity during our time here on earth.

The *Merriam-Webster* dictionary defines honor as: a showing of usually merited respect and esteem to another. Honor is also paralleled with reverence, which implies profound respect, mingled with love, devotion, or awe. God our father is our spiritual parent, and his first commandment is to love and honor him. He then asks us to show the same love and honor to our earthly parents, and when this is done, he will cover us with his grace and mercy, from the crown of our heads to the soles of our feet. We must obey God's word and give honor to our father and mother, even if we feel, for whatever reason, that they don't deserve it. God cannot fulfill his end of his promise to us until we have fulfilled our end of the agreement. Remember: We must have faith in God, hope in his word, and love and honor for him and the vessels he used to bring us into this world. This is the only way to please him and stay worthy of the promises he has for us in this life.

And now these three remain: faith, hope and love. But the greatest of these is love. (1 Corinthians 13:13)

We are living in times wherein parents are spending less quality time with their children; meaning, the children will receive less love and guidance. Whether it is because of their jobs, a need for personal space, or a lack of time, we must realize that God will still hold us accountable for them. Even when we are the innocent victims of parental abuse and neglect, we must still love, care, and pray for them, because when we do this, God will heal us of all the darkness and pain of the past so that we can experience a brighter and longer future on earth and with him.

What We Should Not Do!

The acts of the flesh are obvious: sexual immorality, impurity and debauchery; idolatry and witchcraft;

hatred, discord, jealousy, fits of rage, selfish ambi-
tion, dissensions, factions and envy; drunkenness,
orgies, and the like. I warn you, as I did before, that
those who live like this will not inherit the kingdom
of God. (Galatians 5:19–21)

This scripture simply states that if we continue to do these things, then our souls will not see the promise of heaven, and our earthly blessings will be hindered. God is not playing with us when it comes to these matters. So, it would benefit us greatly if we took this to heart and start cleaning up our act. If we are true believers in his word, then we must realize that God will not tolerate continuous disobedience to his laws without judgment and consequences.

I. Thou shalt not commit idolatry (Exodus 20:3)

When the people saw that Moses was so long in coming down from the mountain, they gathered around Aaron and said, "Come, make us gods who will go before us. As for this fellow Moses who brought us up out of Egypt, we don't know what has happened to him."

Aaron answered them, "Take off the gold earrings that your wives, your sons and your daughters are wearing, and bring them to me."

So, all the people took off their earrings and brought them to Aaron.

He took what they handed him and made it into an idol cast in the shape of a calf, fashioning it with a tool. Then they said, "These are your gods,[b] Israel, who brought you up out of Egypt." (Exodus 32:1–4)

In reflecting on the story of Moses after he led God's people out of Egypt, we find them physically free from slavery but still physically and spiritually lost. They were free to come and go as they please and worship whomever they desired. Although God had delivered them from the clutches of slavery, which they endured for over two hundred years, they still felt the need to have a god they could see with the naked eye. So, they took the gold that they had brought out of Egypt and constructed a golden calf as an idol. This caused God to become so enraged that he told Moses that he would destroy them all. But Moses found favor with him, and he persuaded God to spare their lives.

The major problem that confronts us is the lack of faith in the unseen elements of this world, which are the roots of our spiritual existence. All throughout history, we have tried to find a god, like the people of Israel, that we can see and touch. We have this earthly desire because our flesh needs to make physical contact with the things of this world in order to achieve satisfaction. However, we know that faith is one of the main things we really need to please God, and when he is pleased, we will be blessed.

Unfortunately, we give God the same type of respect today by idolizing the things of this world. We love our spouse, children, parents, homes, cars, clothes, jewelry, careers, money, TV programs, sports teams, and pastors more than we love him. This is in direct violation of the first commandment, which leads us to being guilty of idolatry. Anything that we spend more time with or have more love for is in fact our god.

> For where your treasure is, there your heart will be also. (Matthew 6:21)

Isn't it amazing that we can travel great distances and spend hundreds of dollars in order to attend a concert or sporting event? We jump and shout at these events until we are physically exhausted, but we claim to be too tired to worship God on Sundays. We become irritated at the pastor or praise leader if they ask us to stand and give God a shout of praise for our weekly blessings, but we will jump and shout the moment our favorite entertainer walks out on the stage or one of our superstar players makes a winning play.

When is the last time one of these entertainers or athletes paid our bills, bought us food and clothing, healed and comforted us when we were sick, encouraged us in our moments of depression, helped us mend our broken marriage, or called when someone near and dear to us has passed away? If the answer is never, then why do we give them more praise than we give God and our savior Jesus, who does all of these things and more for us every day? I do not know about you, but I have had a need in all these areas of my life, and the only one that was there for me every time was God and my Lord and savior, Jesus Christ. We can always count on them, and they will supply all our needs.

> *And my God will meet all your needs according to the riches of his glory in Christ Jesus. (Philippians 4:19)*

One day, while watching the local evening news, they aired an interview with a woman from Indiana. She had driven all night to Memphis, Tennessee, in the pouring rain, with her three children and then camped outside the main post office, enduring a light drizzle with hundreds of others, just to buy one of the first Elvis Presley collectable stamps. I think it is fair to say that she, along with hundreds of others, idolize this proclaimed king of rock and roll. Who or what do you worship?

We were made in the spiritual image of God, and it is for this reason that we should follow his word as it pertains to the position or social status of other people. We cannot give more honor to any person or thing than we give to God and his son Jesus. God is no respecter of person, which simply means that he does not consider our wealth, job title or social position, but rather considers the works we do and the amount of faith we possess.

> *But if you show favoritism, you sin and are convicted by the law as lawbreakers. (James 2:9)*

We must strongly consider how much faith we have in and attention we give to others, in relation to the time we spend with our heavenly father. It does not matter whether it is our spouse, children, parents, boss, pastor, close relative, or best friend, we must put

God first and foremost above all others in order to please him. Why? Because he said that he is a jealous god and that he will not expect us to have any other god above him.

> *And God spoke all these words:*
> *"I am the Lord your God, who brought you out of Egypt, out of the land of slavery.*
> *"You shall have no other gods before[a] me.*
> *"You shall not make for yourself an image in the form of anything in heaven above or on the earth beneath or in the waters below.*
> *You shall not bow down to them or worship them; for I, the Lord your God, am a jealous God, punishing the children for the sin of the parents to the third and fourth generation of those who hate me, but showing love to a thousand generations of those who love me and keep my commandments. (Exodus 20:1–6)*

If we truly stop and think about the goodness and mercy of God, along with the never-ending grace that he pours upon our daily lives, then there would be no way for us to consider any other person but God to give our praise, honor, and thanks to. Although we might applaud the efforts of man, we must always remember to praise the blessings of God. He is the only true living idol.

II. Thou shalt not kill. (Exodus 20:13)

Ever since the beginning of time, man has had a problem keeping this commandment. Society looks at this sin as the worst thing a person can do; however, God views it the same as any other transgression.

The first murder recorded was committed by Satan, and the victims were Adam and Eve. God told Adam and Eve that they would die if they ate of the tree of knowledge of good and evil. The devil persuaded Eve, the weaker vessel, to go against the word of God, and she convinced Adam to do the same. This action, to a great degree, killed their spiritual relationship with God, and the result of their actions would follow all future generations, until the resurrection of Jesus Christ. Jesus, known as the second Adam, who died for all our sins, allowing us to be born again spiritually back to the father and restoring the father–son relationship that existed in the beginning.

The Bible records the first act of man taking the life of another in Genesis 4:8. Here we find Cain, one of the sons of Adam and Eve, murdering his brother Abel. He was jealous because God accepted Abel's first fruit offering and rejected his, because he had not given the best that he had to offer. Cain's actions and the spilling of Abel's blood are the reasons God cursed the ground and caused the labor of the land to be difficult, painful, and longsuffering (Genesis 4: 11–12).

God will place judgment on anyone who takes the life of another, and he will also judge those, like Satan, who are out to kill someone's spirit. An abuser, who destroys another's mind and spirit with physical and verbal attacks, must answer to God just like the person who takes another's life. Spiritual and physical death are the same in the eyes of God.

We must stop killing the mind, body, and spirit of others and learn how to give life by building each other up with praise and encouragement, which is drawn from studying the word of God and walking in his wisdom.

III. Thou shalt not commit adultery. (Exodus 20:14)

Since the beginning of time, this sin has been looked upon as a very serious crime against God's holy order. In the Old Testament, people found guilty of this sin where stoned to death by a jury of their peers. Can you imagine being executed by being placed in front of a crowd and having them throw stones at you until you were dead? Sounds pretty barbaric, but that was how they dealt with adultery in man's early days. When Jesus Christ came, he brought a new law that states no one should judge except the father who is in heaven

Do not judge, or you too will be judged. For in the same way you judge others, you will be judged, and with the measure you use, it will be measured to you. (Matthew 7:1–2)

Jesus, at the site of the stoning of Mary Magdalene, a woman accused of adultery, made this statement to her accusers. "When they kept on questioning him, he straightened up and said to them, "Let any one of you who is without sin be the first to throw a stone at her" (John 8:7). Since they all fell short of God's grace and mercy, because of their sin, no stones were cast that day.

God views this sin as a very serious crime against his holy will and the law. However, man's sinful nature has grown to accept it as par for the course in most of today's social circles. Some people even try to justify it by stating that it is just human nature to cheat on our spouse. If it is our sinful nature that causes us to do this, then why would we follow a desire which we know to be wrong in the eyes of God and justify it with worldly reasoning?

The problem God has with this transgression is that it involves breaking a covenant that was made with him on the day we were married. In the presence of God, Jesus, and the Holy Spirit, we publicly stated that we would stay with our spouse under all conditions and forsake all others, until we are parted by death. This is the promise that we made to God concerning our lifelong partner. Once we are joined in marriage, God views the both of us as one person, which is between one man and one woman. There is no biblical record of God honoring same-sex marriage and the one-flesh rule would not apply (view chapters 5 and 10 for further understanding). The reason it is stated that we are one flesh is defined in his word.

That is why a man leaves his father and mother and is united to his wife, and they become one flesh. (Genesis 2:24)

There is a great deal of God-given power in a one-flesh relationship. Whenever two or more people come together for a common purpose with prayer and fall in line with the will of God, then mountains can be moved much easier than it would be by the prayers of one. This is the reason he created the institution of marriage—so that we can experience more power to do things by using our faith and raising our children to believe in God to do the same. It is also the reason the devil hates the union of marriage and will try to use adultery to destroy this holy bond.

We must understand that one Christian is not as powerful as two, which is mainly due to our inherited sinful nature and worldly imperfections. Once God joins two of us together, then we become an unstoppable spiritual force. If adultery destroys a marriage, the judgment of God will come to pass upon the guilty spouse and a lot of the couple's spiritual power is weakened or lost. Furthermore, the families may lose the hedge of protection from worldly problems and situations.

We need to continue to honor God and our spouse by keeping this commandment. We made him a solemn promise, witnessed by family and friends, that we would never forsake one another. If we have the faith to believe that God put us together for life physically, then we need to stay in his will, so we can live together eternally spiritually.

> *Marriage should be honored by all, and the marriage bed kept pure, for God will judge the adulterer and all the sexually immoral. (Hebrews 13:4)*

IV. Thou shall not steal (Exodus 20:15)

This is one of the most frequently broken commandments by Christians and non-Christians alike. The world system has softened the rules on stealing to the point that certain levels of this transgression virtually go unpunished by man. Stealing is done so frequently that it becomes more of a socially accepted way of life than a criminal act. We must remember that stealing anything is a sin against the will of God and, second, and a crime against the law of man.

In the eyes of man, it depends more on what we steal and from whom it is stolen, which will define our degree of punishment. This makes man's law totally out of line with God's will and, therefore, puts man out of line with him as well. When God's natural order is broken, we open the door for Satan to enter and take control of our lives physically and spiritually.

Here are some biblical facts from God's point of view:

A. *God looks at all sin the same. In his eyes sin is sin. "For he who said, "You shall not commit adultery," also said, "You shall not murder." If you do not commit adultery but do commit murder, you have become a lawbreaker (James 2:11)."*

B. *God is no respecter of persons. Who we are and what we do does not give us authority over sin, "[b]ut if you show favoritism, you sin and are convicted by the law as lawbreakers (James 2:9)."*

We have softened our view on stealing so much that we do it unconsciously. Listed are but a few examples of the ways in which we fail in this area:

- Cheating on our income tax returns
- Using company supplies and services for personal use
- Wasting company time while still on the clock
- Knowingly receive the wrong change for a purchase, but fail to return it
- Borrowing money with no intention on repaying the loan
- The items on the bottom of the grocery cart that we forgot to pay for and take them home anyway
- Using the intellectual property of others for self-gain
- Finding a wallet with money, ID, and contact information but never turning it in

Contrary to popular belief, the monetary or material gain as a result of these actions is not some miraculous way in which God decides to bless us. But instead, it is a trick of the enemy trying to get us to willfully fall into a lifestyle of sin and, at the same time, forget our father's rules that govern our lives.

Do we really think that God would take the property of one honest person and give it to us for free when the transaction causes a financial hardship to that property owner? If this were the case, God would have to steal it from them, and that is impossible because he cannot break his own law. Just remember, the devil only takes, but God only gives, and he gives far above what we can envision.

> *The thief comes only to steal and kill and destroy; I have come that they may have life, and have it to the full. (John 10:10)*
>
> *Now to him who is able to do immeasurably more than all we ask or imagine, according to his power that is at work within us. (Ephesians 3:20)*

Remember, stealing comes in many forms. It can be taking someone's material possessions, love, joy, faith, peace, hope, desire, dreams, or sexual innocents. It really doesn't matter in the eyes of the almighty God, so we need to go to him to supply all our needs. Be obedient to the word of God when it comes to the property of others. We should remember the golden rule that states, "Do unto others as you would have them do unto you." It is God's will for us to show as much respect for the property of our neighbor as we would for our own.

> *V. Thou shalt not bear false witness against thou neighbor. (Exodus 20:16)*

Have you ever told a lie? Sure, you have. Everyone has at one time or the other; however, that does not justify the act by any stretch of the imagination, especially when it comes to God's way of thinking. The problem that God has with a lie is that it goes against his word, which is complete truth. There is no gray area with God, because it is either based on total truth or a partial truth, which makes up a whole lie.

Who is responsible for having us think that bending the truth is okay? I think we know the answer, and it is Satan, the father of lies and the author of confusion.

> *You belong to your father, the devil, and you want to carry out your father's desires. He was a murderer from the beginning, not holding to the truth, for there is no truth in him. When he lies, he speaks his native language, for he is a liar and the father of lies. (John 8:44)*

The devil's sole purpose is to keep us so confused with the truth that we can no longer distinguish it from an ungodly reality. The true reality is what God's law states about the way we should live and how we should treat our fellow man.

> *In fact, everyone who wants to live a godly life in Christ Jesus will be persecuted, 13 while evildoers and impostors will go from bad to worse, deceiving and being deceived. (2 Timothy 3:12–13)*

There is no untruth that will not surface sooner or later. All lies are hidden in the heart, a place God knows all about, which makes it impossible for us to hide anything from him. This one area of sin is holding so many of us back spiritually, because we think that getting away with a lie is fine as long as we don't get caught by man. However, man is the least of our worries when it comes to answering for the wrong that is a result of untruth. This is especially true when it is done against one of God's own children.

Think of it this way: If someone beat up the neighbor's kid, we may feel bad for the child and probably show concern for his or her well-being. However, if the same thing happens to our own child, then our feelings would surely change. God feels the same way toward his children, which are those of us who are saved by the blood of Jesus Christ, the true son of God. Anyone who is saved is considered to be a child of God and one of his disciples.

*To the Jews who had believed him, Jesus said, "If
you hold to my teaching, you are really my disciples.
Then you will know the truth, and the truth will set
you free." (John 8:31–32)*

Learn to turn away from the darkness of lies and walk in the
light of truth, because the truth will set us free.

*If we claim to have fellowship with him and yet walk
in the darkness, we lie and do not live out the truth.
But if we walk in the light, as he is in the light, we
have fellowship with one another, and the blood of
Jesus, his Son, purifies us from all sin. 1 John 1:6–7*

*VI. Thou shalt not covet anything that is thy neigh-
bors. (Exodus 20:17)*

The word covet is not frequently used in our daily conversa-
tions, so I felt it necessary to supply more insight into its actual meaning. The dictionary defines covet as follows: (1) to wish or desire for
enviously. (2) to wish, long, or hope for, with the painful or resentful
awareness of an advantage enjoyed by another, along with the desire
to possess the same advantage. That's deep!

Now, we can see that to covet is not just something we do but
also the way that we think. It is the seed of other sins, which can
grow out of control without the necessary spiritual strength needed
to choke it out. Before we can kill, steal, or commit adultery, we start
first by coveting the person or object in our hearts and minds. If
this desire is held onto long enough, it will turn into a physical act.
Coveting was conceived with the initial desiring thought and sin was
born with the action that followed.

*Keep your lives free from the love of money and be
content with what you have, because God has said,
"Never will I leave you; never will I forsake you."
(Hebrews 13:5)*

This is the reason we forget to repent for coveting, because most of the time, we are not even aware that we are doing anything wrong. From the creation of man, coveting has been one of the main ingredients of our sins. Some past and present examples of this are the following:

- Eve's desire for the knowledge of good and evil.
- Moses's desire to revenge treatment of his friend
- King David's desire for Bathsheba, General Urethra's wife
- Solomon and Samson's desire for women outside of their faith
- Lot's daughter's desire to have a child by their father
- Abraham's desire for a son before God blessed his seed with his wife Sarah
- President Clinton's desire for his young aid, Monica Lewinsky
- Bernard Madoff's greed for money using a Ponzi scheme
- Adolf Hitler's quest for power and control of the world
- Archangel Lucifer's (now called Satan) desire to be the chosen heir of God
- Donald Trump's desire to be President of the United States, but no godly desire to be humble enough to unify the nation.

All of these examples speak of individuals who fell into the trap of coveting something that was not theirs to possess. All of them paid a price for their sinful actions.

Apostle Paul's dilemma:

I do not understand what I do. For what I want to do I do not do, but what I hate I do. (Romans 7:15)

Apostle Paul was handpicked by God because of his unwavering faith. He was a Jew and he strongly followed the law to the letter. The teachings of Jesus Christ brought about changes to the old teachings and the birth of his followers known as Christians. Paul loved God with all his mind, body, and soul but, with equal passion, hated the Christians who followed the new law that Jesus had established. He tortured and killed them at every opportunity.

God chose Paul because of this love and devotion that he possessed. He knew that when he changed Paul's heart to the new law, he would be one of the greatest apostles of all time. When Paul was on the road to Damascus to seek out these blasphemers of the Jewish faith called Christians and kill them, Jesus spoke to him out loud and asked why he was persecuting him. He caused Paul to go blind and to meet a man named Ananias, who would change his life forever.

God used his servant Paul, because he was strong in his faith and he knew that if Paul came over to the side of the new law, he would be unstoppable. Yet, Paul, with all of his unwavering faith, could not stop from sinning.

Sinful thoughts flood our mind all the time, but only by the grace and mercy from God can strength be found to overcome these temptations. There is a special reward for every time we refuse to yield to the sinful thoughts.

> *Blessed is the one who perseveres under trial because, having stood the test, that person will receive the crown of life that the Lord has promised to those who love him. (James 1:12)*

If we can grab hold of Paul's insight, we would understand that we are at odds not only with the world but also with ourselves. It is very important that we understand how to take control of our flesh, because it is always seeking satisfaction by way of Satan's worldly vices, and our flesh will try to reach this goal by any means necessary. We must learn to live within the provisions of God's blessings. If we can learn to do that, our need for the world's pleasures will subside.

Summary:

Let us do a recap of the ten important life-saving rules.

A. The four things we *should* do:

1. Love God first, with all our being
2. Love others as yourself
3. Honor the Sabbath day
4. Honor our Mother and Father.

B. The six things we should not do:

1. Do not worship other idols
2. Do not kill
3. Do not steal
4. Do not commit adultery
5. Do not lie
6. Do not covet anything or anyone

There we have it, all of God's rules of this game called life. We need to read them over and over until we hold them to memory. Then, we need to make an earnest effort to live by them daily, and this will help us develop a healthier heart and spirit. Living by the rules will help us control our flesh. It is the flesh that seeks the pleasures of the world, which will bring death to the spirit by way of these physical transgressions.

A child goes into the kitchen and takes a handful of cookies to carry to their room. If the parents find out and confront the child to punish them for their actions but never told the child that this was wrong or forbidden, then the punishment would not be fair or just. However, once the child is instructed to stay out of the cookie jar and does it anyway, then correction is justified.

God expects the same obedience from us when it pertains to these rules of the game. After we accept Jesus as our Lord and savior, and we are at the age of mental and spiritual maturity, then we will be held accountable for our actions. Repentance is the only thing that will get us off the hook with God. He has spiritual X-ray vision that can see our true heart, so if we ask for forgiveness and are not totally sincere, then our sin will not be forgiven.

We have tried living the world's way, so now, try living it God's way. His way is the truth and the truth will always set us *free*. Godly obedience will help us cut down on the need for spiritual first aid, but when we do take an unexpected fall, his healing power is in our repentance for the transgression. He is only a prayer away.

Prayer for Keeping the Law

Dear God and most gracious heavenly father, we come before you, asking that you allow your word and your laws to be written in our hearts. Bring all things concerning your will to our remembrance so that it will meet us at the point of our need. You stated in your word that repentance is the key to forgiveness, so please accept our words. We are truly sorry for our sins and ask that you will cleanse us and make us whole again. These blessings we ask in the mighty name of your son Jesus Christ. Amen.

Key Scriptures

Please read the entire chapter of each verse for greater edification and understanding.

1. *James 2:10*
2. *John 8:44*
3. *Matthew 22:37*
4. *1 John 4:12*
5. *John 14:15*
6. *John 3:16*
7. *Matthew 22:38*
8. *Psalm 133:1*
9. *Proverbs 10:12*

10. *Luke 10: 29–37*
11. *Exodus 20:8*
12. *(1 Timothy 6: 10)*
13. *Job 36:11*
14. *Mark 2:27*
15. *Exodus 20:12*
16. *1 Corinthians 13:13*
17. *Galatians 5:19–21*
18. *Exodus 20:3*
19. *Exodus 32:1–4*
20. *Matthew 6:21*
21. *Philippians: 4:19*
22. *James 2:9*
23. *Exodus 20:1–6*
24. *Exodus 20:13*
25. *Genesis 4:11–12*
26. *James 2:8–9*
27. *Exodus 20:14*
28. *Matthew 7:1–2*
29. *John 8:12*
30. *Genesis 2:24*
31. *Hebrews 13:4*
32. *Exodus 20:15*
33. *James 2:11*
34. *James 2:9*
35. *John 10:10*
36. *Ephesians 3:20*
37. *Matthew 7:12*
38. *John 8:7*
39. *John 8:44*
40. *2 Timothy 3:12–13*
41. *John 8:31–32*
42. *John 1:6–7*
43. *Exodus 20:17*
44. *Hebrews 13:5*
45. *Romans 7:15*

CHAPTER THREE

Path to Temptation

"See no evil, hear no evil, speak no evil." This phrase has been around forever and holds a great deal of godly truth within its context. The world presents us with the temptation to sin through that which we see, hear and speak. Although we feel in control of these three senses most of the time, a lot of it can still bypass our personal filters during our normal daily activities.

> *Blessed is the one who perseveres under trial because, having stood the test, that person will receive the crown of life that the Lord has promised to those who love him. (James 1:12)*

Temptation is the main tool that the devil uses against us, because it concerns desires of the flesh. Man is made up of spirit and flesh, which was created by God. Our flesh, which was transformed from earthly clay, is what God used to create our earthly vessels. The words "earth" and "world" are synonymous; therefore, they are one and the same. This is the reason we are an earthly being with a worldly nature. The archangel Lucifer and his fellow angels, who are now called Satan and his demons, were cast out of heaven to dwell on earth to rule it and its inhabitants. God cannot destroy them and they cannot die. Having established this connection between the earthly realm and Satan, we can start to understand why we are so weak to the desires of the flesh. The fact that this occured before the creation of man caused the earth to inherit a sinful nature and its ground to be corrupt.

> *The great dragon was hurled down—that ancient serpent called the devil, or Satan, who leads the whole world astray. He was hurled to the earth, and his angels with him.*
>
> *Therefore rejoice, you heavens and you who dwell in them! But woe to the earth and the sea, because the devil has gone down to you! He is filled with fury, because he knows that his time is short. (Revelation 12:9, 12)*

The things of this world are under the same curse, thus producing the sinful nature of man. This is why we describe someone who lives in a sinful manner as being a worldly person.

We are made up of three elements: spirit that has a soul and lives in a body made of flesh. The spirit and flesh are constantly at war with one another over which one will control our soul. The spirit–man wants to please God while the flesh just wants to satisfy itself by way of worldly pleasures and habitual vices.

> *Whoever loves pleasure will become poor; whoever loves wine and olive oil will never be rich. (Proverbs 21:17)*

We all know wealthy sinners. However, the wealth that is spoken of here is not physical but rather spiritual. We must make it our goal to build up and strengthen the spirit–man within us so that it can help control the desires of our flesh. If we do not possess this spiritual control in our lives, the flesh will surely lead us down a path of self-destruction and spiritual bankruptcy.

> *When tempted, no one should say, "God is tempting me." For God cannot be tempted by evil, nor does he tempt anyone; but each person is tempted when*

they are dragged away by their own evil desire and enticed. Then, after desire has conceived, it gives birth to sin; and sin, when it is full-grown, gives birth to death. (James 1:13–15)

1. *See no evil*

For everything in the world—the lust of the flesh, the lust of the eyes, and the pride of life—comes not from the Father but from the world. (1 John 2:16)

The eyes take in a tremendous amount of information every day. We awake in the morning and look outside to see if it is sunny or cloudy, which will generally influence our initial perception of our whole day. A sunny day leads us to believe the day will bring joy and good fortune, while gray skies leads way to feelings of mild despair. All of this emotional baggage can come with a simple view of the daily weather conditions. Our visual outlook of our surroundings, to a large degree, controls our basic view or perception of the world as a whole. In this case, "What we see is what we get" becomes our daily motto. We, who are members of the body of Christ, will quickly confess that this self-perceived motto is totally false. "For we live by faith, not by sight" (*2 Corinthians 5:7*).

In Paul's declaration to the church of Corinth, he lets them know that they could not live their lives making decisions based solely on what they can perceive with the naked eye. Rather, they must trust completely in the word of God to be their daily guide. So, we must use our eyes to do the same by enjoying God's marvelous creations and praise him for the sunshine and the rain, because they both serve a divine purpose.

When Jesus spoke again to the people, he said, "I am the light of the world. Whoever follows me will never walk in darkness, but will have the light of life." (John 8:12)

We know the world can be a very dark place and the only way we can defeat darkness is with light. This is why God sent his son Jesus Christ to be our spiritual guide and to show us the way in the midst of this earthly darkness. This is the main reason we must control the amount of worldly darkness that we take in through what we watch, because darkness and light cannot exist in the same place. We must continue to walk by faith in God and not by our worldly vision. If we use our God-given wisdom, along with the spiritual vision that he has given us, then we will not suffer the physical and spiritual wounds that come as a result of sinning with our eyes.

2. *Hear no evil*

   The way of fools seems right to them, but the wise listen to advice. (Proverbs 12:15)

   Consequently, faith comes from hearing the message, and the message is heard through the word about Christ. (Romans 10:17)

What we hear can greatly affect us emotionally. Mellow sounds give us a sense of calmness, while loud banging and crashing noises tend to make us tense, irritable, and edgy. Soft-spoken words of encouragement boost our spirits, creating a sense of joy and inner peace, while loud words of criticism destroy our self-confidence, making us feel stressed, depressed and defeated. These are but a few examples of the type of sounds that we hear every day, and for the most part, they are out of our control. So, we are left to just listen and react, hopefully in a positive manner, to what we take in.

It would be very hard to function in this world without being able to communicate through our hearing. If we can hear another person speak and still misunderstand the information that they've given us, then think how difficult it must be to live without being able to hear anything at all. Communication is the key to our overall success in life. What we hear as well as the interpretation of it will determine the general course of action that will follow.

My dear brothers and sisters, take note of this:
Everyone should be quick to listen, slow to speak and
slow to become angry. (James 1:19)

It would be extremely wise of us to take more time in becoming a more effective listener and using this godly wisdom to discern what we hear before we react. Not only is this great advice but also, by James's own account, it's within the will of God to do so. As the stories in the Bible tell us, nobody has ever seen God, but many have heard his voice. It was through his holy speaking that we were able to receive his godly instruction and his people were able to write these words that we are reading from the Bible today.

Even today, God still speaks to us. He does not speak from a burning bush, like he spoke to Moses, but rather through our conscience, with the understanding coming from the *Holy Spirit that dwells within our hearts.* This is how God inspired me to write this book. If we are not in tune to his voice, then we cannot hear him, and our diagnosis would be that we are spiritually deaf and dumb to his gospel or words.

My people are destroyed from lack of knowledge.
"Because you have rejected knowledge, I also reject you
as my priests; because you have ignored the law of your
God, I also will ignore your children. (Hosea 4:6)

Likewise, God's ability to hear us is also based on our relationship with him. If we do not have a relationship with God, including our praise for our daily blessings, some form of individual worship, personal study of the word, and obedience of his laws, then he cannot hear our prayers. Therefore, they would have been spoken in vain. It is like trying to talk to someone on our cell phone when they are out of range. We can hear ourselves talk but the other party cannot. It is the exact same way with God, because if we are not living in line with his word, we lose that holy signal. Spiritually, we have traveled outside of his calling area.

The fact of the matter is that we will be driven to do all kinds of things in this life by an inner voice, which may or may not be from God. If our relationship with him is weak, then we may not recognize his voice when he is speaking. We could in fact be listening to the voice of Satan. Let's clean out our spiritual ears of the worldly wisdom from Satan so that they will be open to hear what God is saying to us through his word. It might be the very words that we need to heal our spirits and save our soul.

3. *Speak no evil*

> *For, "Whoever would love life and see good days*
> *must keep their tongue from evil and their lips from*
> *deceitful speech. (1 Peter 3:10)*

Have we ever said something that hurt someone's feelings and immediately wish we could take it back? For most of us, this is a moment that we wish could erased, but unfortunately, that is impossible to do. The tongue is a very powerful tool, and it needs to be spiritually monitored while in use. We can create great joy in someone's life with our words of love and praise, or we can speak words full of criticism and hate that will literally start wars.

> *And the tongue also is a fire, a world of evil among*
> *the parts of the body. It corrupts the whole body, sets*
> *the whole course of one's life on fire, and is itself set*
> *on fire by hell. (James 3:6)*

We must learn to guard the actions of our tongue. If we don't, then we will slowly lose control of the spiritual atmosphere around us. The results of such a loss will come at a great cost, which could be the collapse of our marriage, the loss of respect from our children, termination from our job, expulsion from school, loss of a position at our church and even removal from political office, just to name a few.

As a parent of four, I've noticed a change in the way children today talk to their parents and other adult figures. The tone they use when they speak and the things they say are starting to become more disrespectful. This is not a serious problem in my home, but it is a growing one in our society because this action is out of the will of God, and any action that is not in his will must be condemned. When God condemns anything, a curse will follow this action.

> *Honor your father and your mother, so that you may*
> *live long in the land the Lord your God is giving*
> *you. (Exodus 20:12)*

If this matter of children dishonoring their parents continues, we will start to notice God's word coming to pass as the death rate of the young increases due to things that never existed in the past. They will lose the protective hedge that God placed around them. Children are dying in increasing numbers from STD (sexual transmitted diseases), abuse, addictions, heart attacks, diabetes, cancer, accidents and suicide. Once God's word has gone forth, it cannot return void. He does not take the life of a child because of their disrespect; rather, it is a consequence for their failure to follow the godly instructions from their parents.

> *"So is my word that goes out from my mouth: It will*
> *not return to me empty, but will accomplish what*
> *I desire and achieve the purpose for which I sent it"*
> *(Isaiah 55:11).*

The older generations are not excused from this law of using words against their parents either. We used to care for our elderly parents in our homes when they became unable to do so for themselves. Now, they are warehoused in insensitive, over-priced nursing homes by less-than-loving caregivers and, in some cases, become the victims of physical, sexual, and mental abuse. If we notice, while health care has improved to help us live longer, we too are dying younger at higher rates from illnesses which used to only be among the elderly. Again, the word of God has to prevail. Yes, this is just words that we are speaking, but the reality is that words have great power, whether used for good or bad. The outcome of the words spoken is predestined, along with the judgment for the one who spoke them.

Families are the key elements of the world, and the devil knows it. This is why there is so much confusion in the home. If godly order is not restored in the home system, then society will continue to deteriorate as a result. There is an absence of God-fearing, Christian fathers who love, honor, and respect their wives in front of their children. When parents do not take their children to church, pray with them, or present themselves as living examples of godly living, then the family system is predestined to fail. This system must be fixed in order to heal this spiritually sick society.

> *You will hear of wars and rumors of wars, but see to it that you are not alarmed. Such things must happen, but the end is still to come. (Matthew 24:6)*

Words have even been used throughout time to start wars. When we look at the war in Iraq, we realize that it was started because of an unproven rumor about the presence of weapons of mass destruction. Although these weapons were never discovered or any real evidence of the locations of their fabrication, the war of words prevailed, and our President, George W. Bush, decided that war was the only course of action.

As of September 2014, the number of American lives lost to this war totaled 4,486 along with hundreds of thousands with life-changing injuries. This, along with the deaths of many, many innocent Iraqi citizens, and we still do not know the real reason for this war other than a great failure to communicate information. If we were to pose the question of why we were fighting in Iraq to fifty people, we would get close to fifty different answers, which means America is still in a state of confusion on this issue.

> *For God is not a God of disorder but of peace—as in all the congregations of the Lord's people. (1 Corinthians 14:33)*

If this confusion did not come from God, then where did it originate?

> *You belong to your father, the devil, and you want to carry out your father's desires. He was a murderer from the beginning, not holding to the truth, for there is no truth in him. When he lies, he speaks his native language, for he is a liar and the father of lies. (John 8:44)*

The devil is the author of confusion, and he is very good at it. He can get us to use our words to do his will, whenever we are out of the will of God. So, we need to remember again the words of James who said, "My dear brothers and sisters, take note of this: Everyone should be quick to listen, slow to speak and slow to become angry." This is the key to using godly wisdom when we speak.

We are living in the age of communication. There are many talk shows that fill the airways with all forms of information. Some of this information is useful while the majority of it has no useful purpose for our lives whatsoever. With the aid of satellites, most television programs can be viewed anywhere in the world. The Internet, which gives us access to any kind of data by way of the World Wide Web, e-mail, chat rooms, Facebook, Instagram, and Twitter, are in full force. Also, the cell-phone industry has grown into one of the largest industries in the world, which makes it easy to keep in touch with others at all times.

As the world has become smaller with the use of these new forms of communication, the devil has been busy perverting this medium at every turn. We have seen talk shows like Morton Downey Jr., Jerry Springer, Steve Wilkos, Maury Povich and Howard Stern, pornography on the Internet, sex offenders using chat rooms to arrange their meetings, and prepaid cell phones and calling cards used as a way to hide affairs and other criminal activity. We must take control of what goes into our hearts and minds by using God's wisdom to discern good from evil.

Two famous songwriters, Thom Bell and Linda Creed, wrote a secular love song entitled, "Stop, Look, and Listen (listen to our heart and hear what it is saying)." God wants us to do the same as spoken in the words of this song concerning his holy word. Stop to spend time with him and his word. Look at ourselves to see if we are truly serving him like we should. Finally, listen to our heart so we can hear what he is saying, and he will direct our path. Once we learn to stop, look, and listen to his voice, then the spiritual healing process will start to take place in our lives. God will then use us and answer our prayers as he did for his servant Jabez.

The Pray of Jabez

> Jabez cried out to the God of Israel, "Oh, that you would bless me and enlarge my territory! Let your hand be with me, and keep me from harm so that I will be free from pain." And God granted his request.(1 Chronicles 4:10)

We must remember that temptation is how we become spiritually infected, but resisting temptation is the cure and the key to God's blessings.

A Prayer for Forgiveness

O Lord, as we look into our lives, we see much that displeases you. We know that we have sinned, and our sin is against you and our neighbor. Our sins stand before us now and they are placing a hedge between us. We are not happy as we should be nor able to rejoice as we want to. So, we come with repentance and faith, asking for your forgiveness. You promised that if we confess our sins, You will forgive us and cleanse us from them. So, we ask for forgiveness and cleansing. Help us to conform to your will and grant that we have a likeness unto Christ. Give us strength as we face daily temptations and cover us with your divine grace and mercy. You are a forgiver of sin, so come into our hearts to convict us each time we would turn away from you. We ask this in the name of Jesus Christ, our Lord and savior and for his sake. Amen.

Key Scriptures

Please read the entire chapter of each verse for greater edification and understanding.

1. *James 1:12*
2. *Revelation 12:9–12*
3. *Proverbs 21:17*
4. *James 1:13–15*
5. *1 John 2:16*
6. *2 Corinthians 5:7*
7. *John 8:12*
8. *Proverbs 12:15*
9. *Romans 10:17*
10. *James 1:19*
11. *Hosea 4:6*
12. *1 Peter 3:10*
13. *James 3:6*
14. *Exodus 20:12*
15. *Isaiah 55:11*
16. *Matthew 24:6*
17. *1 Corinthians 14:33*
18. *John 9:44*
19. *1 Chronicles 4:10*

CHAPTER FOUR

It's Time to Sing a New Song
The Power of Words

I n music, we generally find that it reflects the thinking of the generation during the times in which we live. If music is truly a product of our heart and soul, then many of today's lyricist seem to have become dark and void of godly passion. This passion that inspires the words and rhythms of these melodious creations possess the ability to sooth the savage beast or cause it to do deeds of evil.

We hear it all the time, how some of the music produced by the young artist today is causing their fan base to be violent, rebellious, and promiscuous. I do not agree with every argument directed at today's music and that it is having a negative impact on society, but it is definitely moving quickly in an ungodly direction.

> *Therefore, get rid of all moral filth and the evil that is so prevalent and humbly accept the word planted in you, which can save you. (James 1:21)*

As I reflect on the songs that I heard growing up, I realize that there are some that have a rhythmic beat I still enjoy, but the words are no longer pleasing to my spirit. This is because what the artist is saying is out of the will of God. Their words are not in line with godly thinking and his will for our lives. The more we take in God's word, the less room we hold in our hearts for worldly input.

Let me tell you the story of two men, who became multimillionaires by using the rhythm of the same song but with different words that changed the outcome of their lives. The first gentleman who wrote this song was James Ambrose Johnson, born on February 1, 1948, in Buffalo, New York, and known to us as Rick James.

Mr. James was the leader of a group, under the Motown recording label, called Rick James and the Stone City Band. This group was extremely popular around the late '70s and early '80s, with such hit songs as "Mary Jane," Fire and Desire," and their most popular song "Super Freak." The first selection, "Mary Jane," was a slow-tempo dance tune that spoke of the author's love for getting high on Mary Jane, which was a nickname for marijuana during the time. The second selection, "Fire and Desire," a love duet with fellow singer, the late Teena Marie (March 5, 1956–December 26, 2010), dealt with a love affair between two people who were compatible because they used, abused, and mistreated all their prior love interests. But the song that brought Mr. James his greatest success was the famous up-tempo dance hit "Super Freak." This selection was a huge hit on radio and dance clubs all over the free world. This song had a great beat and with sexy lyrics that made it very easy to follow and hard to forget.

The words of this song spoke of a young lady who was sexually kinky, which won her the title of a super freak. She loved to hang out with the boys in the band and do whatever, wherever with whoever desired her at the time. She was basically a sex slave without physical shackles. As I mentioned, there is tremendous power in the spoken word of God and also in his final creation, man. We must realize that we will be held accountable for every word we utter from our lips.

This is a sample of the words from the first verse of the song "Super Freak":

> She's a very kinky girl,
> The kind you don't take home to mother
> She will never let your spirits down,
> Once you get her off the street.

She likes the boys in the band,
She says that I'm her all-time favorite
When I make my move to her room
It's the right time, she's never hard to please.

That girl is pretty wild now
The girl's a super freak
The kind of girl you read about
In the new-wave magazines.
That girl is pretty kinky
The girl's a super freak
I really like to taste her
Every time we meet.
She's all right, she's all right
That girl's all right with me, yeah.

In 1991, Rick James, at the age of forty-three, was convicted of assaulting a woman. The attack, which he committed with his twenty-one-year-old live-in girlfriend Tanya Ann Hijazi, stated that they picked up a twenty-six-year-old woman from a party, held her against her will for over six days. While tied to a chair, she was burned with a hot knife and crack pipe, then forced to perform sexual acts during a cocaine binge at his West Hollywood home. He was released from prison in 1996 but was once again accused of sexually assaulting a music executive, Mary Sauger, at the St James Club on Sunset Strip, but the charges were later dropped.

Mr. James, who seemed to be on a constant quest for the super freak in his life, served around five years while Ms. Hijazi served fifteen months for the crimes. They wanted the two women to be their personal super freaks against their will, and subsequently paid the price. Rick James was later sued in civil court for two-million dollars by Ms. Sauger, leaving him bankrupt.

A good person leaves an inheritance for their children's children, but a sinner's wealth is stored up for the righteous. (Proverbs 13:22)

In 1999, Rick James, after serving his sentence, was in the process of resuming his career when he had a stroke, which was accredited to a condition known as rock-and-roll neck. It is caused by the rapid back-and-forth motions some rock-and-roll musicians make when they perform, which weakens blood vessels in the neck. The blood vessels become weak enough to break, stopping the blood flow to the brain. He seemed to be doing fairly well during the recovery period, with the exception of a slight limp. Mr. James passed in his sleep on August 6, 2004, in Burbank, California, of heart failure.

The second gentleman is Mr. Stanley Kirk Burrell, born March 30, 1962, in Oakland, California, whose show name is MC Hammer. He started his career entertaining fans with his dance moves in the parking lot of the NFL team Oakland Raiders. As the popularity of rap music grew in the late '80s and early '90s, MC Hammer formed a group with a full band and dancers, which was an unusual move for a rap artist. The majority of rap groups at the time performed with just a PA system for the vocals and two turntables to supply the background musical accompaniment. M C Hammer's well-rehearsed group hit the concert circuit with a bang and set the rap world on fire, along with building a huge crossover market.

MC Hammer's hit song was "U Can't Touch This," which brought forth a positive motivating message about being self-confident. The beat and rhythm of this hit song was the same as that of the Rick James's hit "Super Freak" but with a totally different message.

Here are some of the lyrics to: "U Can't Touch This"

> Can't touch this (repeat five times)
> My, my, my, my music hits me so hard
> Makes me say "Oh, my Lord"
> Thank you for blessing me
> With a mind to rhyme and two hype feet
> It feels good when you know you're down
> A super dope homeboy from the Oaktown
> And I'm known as such
> And this is a beat, uh, u can't touch

MC Hammer's second hit single was titled "2 Legit 2 Quit," which was written as a response to other rap artists who were saying that he was not a legitimate rapper and labeled him as a copycat entertainer. By the mid '90s, MC Hammer stopped touring due to cash flow problems, which were a result of a drop in record sales and the high cost associated with the elaborate stage production. After being sued by Rick James over the unauthorized use of his song "Super Freak," along with many bad private investments and poor money management; Mr. Hammer had to file for bankruptcy as well.

MC Hammer is touring again with some of his faithful past band members, and he is now a minister spreading the gospel through word, song and dance.

> *Praise him with the sounding of the trumpet, praise him with the harp and lyre, praise him with timbrel and dancing, praise him with the strings and pipe, praise him with the clash of cymbals, praise him with resounding cymbals. Let everything that has breath praise the Lord. Praise the Lord. (Psalm 150: 3–6)*

As mentioned in the beginning of this chapter, the youth culture of today is affected by the music they entertain, just as Rick James and MC Hammer were affected by their own creations. Rick James created a song with a great rhythm and beat but a worldly message, thus leading him into a worldly, sin-centered lifestyle that tarnished his reputation and contributed to his untimely demise. On the other hand, MC Hammer used the same popular rhythm but with a positive message that falls within the will of God and encourages us to rise above worldly conditions and public judgment. He took his own divine advice and overcame his own personal demons to serve God. Now, he is very much alive, serving God and walking in holy wisdom within his career.

Let us learn from these two gentlemen and be mindful of what we say, how we speak, as well as what we listen too. We must remember that whatever we take in through our senses is added to the heart and mind like a camera recording onto a tape or disk. The only way for us to overcome the negative input of the past is to overwrite it with the word of God. Otherwise, it will stay with us forever.

There are two important things we should remember from the word of God:

> First, "A good man brings good things out of the good stored up in his heart, and an evil man brings evil things out of the evil stored up in his heart. For the mouth speaks what the heart is full of" (Luke 6:45).
>
> Second, "The tongue also is a fire, a world of evil among the parts of the body. It corrupts the whole body, sets the whole course of one's life on fire, and is itself set on fire by hell" (James 3:6)

There is an old saying that states: "Sticks and stones can break my bones, but words can never hurt me." This statement holds some truth from a physical standpoint, but spiritually speaking, it is the prefect lie. Words can harm us if we are not spiritually strong. Therefore, we must feed on God's word daily to build up this spiritual immune system to a degree that we no longer feel pain or anger from verbal attacks of the world.

As we grow spiritually, we must allow the word of God to renew our minds, which will help us change our hearts and, in turn, aid us in controlling our tongue. Once we control our tongue, then our words will become more in line with God's will and divine purpose for our lives.

Apostle James stated in chapter three, verse six that we will never be in complete control of our tongues because to do so would mean physical perfection. However, we should always be mindful of its power when we use it and try to speak that which is good. Let us season our words with the fruit of the spirit, which are love, joy, peace, longsuffering, gentleness, goodness, faith, meekness, and temperance. If we do this, our words will plant godly seeds in the minds and hearts of the receiver. This will truly please God and allow more blessings to flow into our life as well as the lives of others.

Above all else, guard your heart, for everything you
do flows from it. (Proverbs 4:23)

We need to practice what we preach and watch what we speak. This way, we will cause less pain and suffering to others, as well as, creating a healthier spiritual environment around us. Jesus said: "What goes into someone's mouth does not defile them, but what comes out of their mouth, that is what defiles them" (Matthew 15:11).

A Prayer for Our Words

Our father, who has been our provider and sustainer from the beginning, we praise your holy name. We thank you for the blessings of mercy and grace that we are so fortunate to awake to every day. We humbly ask you to forgive us of the transgressions that we have committed through our spoken words. Although we cannot take back these words, it is our heartfelt desire that you can instill in us your spirit, so we will not offend them with our words again. And help them to forgive us for the lack of control of our tongue. Let the words of my mouth and the meditations of my heart be acceptable in thy sight, O, Lord, my strength and my Redeemer. In the holy name of Jesus, we pray. Amen.

Key Scriptures

Please read the entire chapter of each verse for greater edification and understanding.

1. *James 1:21*
2. *Proverbs 13:22*
3. *Psalm 150: 3–6*
4. *Luke 6:45*
5. *James 3:6*
6. *Proverbs 4:23*

CHAPTER FIVE

Contract for Life

T his is a subject that's near and dear to the hearts of many of us today. It concerns a lifelong contract that some of us made or plan to make with God and someone we truly love. This contract is quite different than most. The terms of the agreement must be spoken aloud in public, and it has to be witnessed by two or more people. These witnesses are asked by the contract reader if they, for any reason, feel this agreement between the two of you should not go forward; their remarks can stop the process.

For the benefit of those who have not figured it out, this is the contract of marriage or holy matrimony. The problem with this contract is that people forget about three very important witnesses who are also present at almost all of these contractual agreements. They are God the father, Jesus his son, and the Holy Spirit, also known together as the Holy Trinity. When these three are present during this public announcement, it adds a spiritual dynamic to the agreement process. The reason it was stated in almost all of the marriage services is because the Holy Trinity is not present for this ceremony if we are not born-again believers or are couples of the same sex (review chapter 10).

If the Holy Trinity is present, then we are not only making this agreement with the other person, but more importantly, we are making a covenant with them. Once these three are made a part of the contractual arrangement, the rules of the world-based agreement change, and it then becomes a spiritual-and-physical contract binding the two until death. Also, a marriage must be consummated to make it complete in the eyes of God and legal by men's law. This is another reason God does not accept same-sex marriage.

> *Do not have sexual relations with a man as one does*
> *with a woman; that is detestable. (Leviticus 18:22)*

My wife and I have been married for over thirty years, and we renew our wedding vows every five. This is something that she wanted us to do, but not without some initial objection on my part. However, after thirty-four years and four wonderful children later, I realized that being reminded of this covenant agreement, which I made with her, God, Jesus, and the Holy Spirit, will add new life and strength to the commitment that we have to this promise of lifelong devotion.

Let's examine a few facts that form the basis for a godly union. First, God created man and then with a rib from man, he created a help meet for him called woman. Man, by definition of the word means, male and woman is defined as female, because she was made from man.

The Lord God said, "It is not good for the man to be alone. I will make a helper suitable for him."

> *So the Lord God caused the man to fall into a deep*
> *sleep; and while he was sleeping, he took one of the*
> *man's ribs and then closed up the place with flesh.*
> *Then the Lord God made a woman from the rib he*
> *had taken out of the man, and he brought her to*
> *the man.*
>
> *The man said, "This is now bone of my bones*
> *and flesh of my flesh; she shall be called 'woman,' for*
> *she was taken out of man." That is why a man leaves*
> *his father and mother and is united to his wife, and*
> *they become one flesh. (Genesis 2:18, 21–24)*

This was the first marriage, because they were created together by God from one flesh. It is for this reason that we consider the holy ceremonial marriage between a *man* and a *woman* a one-flesh union. This is the relationship of two individuals of the *opposite sex,* joined physically into one flesh spiritually and consummated physically. If this union is not done in the presence of God, Jesus, and the Holy Spirit, then the fact of becoming one flesh will not exist and neither will the blessing of a one-flesh relationship. There is tremendous spiritual power that exists within the body of a one-flesh relationship. God will show favor over the union, and blessings will be available to the both of you. In order to open the pipeline of God's blessings, we must keep our end of the agreement. We must uphold the contract terms, because if we do not, then blessings will stop flowing and the hedge of protection disappears.

If we think back to chapter two concerning the Ten Commandments and what will happen if we forget them, then the same thing can occur within our marriage. The fact that my wife and I renew our union vows every five years helps us remember the terms of our contract with the Holy Trinity and one another. This is also good for the marriages of the families and friends who attend the renewal service, because they can also rethink their moment of commitment or reconsider the terms for their own future plans. We must realize one very important fact, and that is when we repeat the wedding vows, we are not speaking to one another, but we are making a promise and covenant with the Holy Trinity.

Let's review the parts of this contract and bring to our attention the importance of the words being spoken in the presence of God and the witnesses.

The following are traditional wedding vows:

> *We promise to be faithful to one another, in good times and in bad, in sickness and in health, for richer or poorer, to love and honor one another and forsake all others, all the days of our life, until death do us part.*

Have you ever known a couple who lived together outside the covenant of marriage? They seem, for the most part, happy and content. Living together outside of marriage is totally out of the will of God, but we find a lot of Christians today settling for this rather comfortable relationship. How can we consider ourselves a true child of God and have such blatant disregard for his law? We must realize that there are serious consequences to being disobedient in this area of our lives.

> *Now for the matters you wrote about: "It is good for a man not to have sexual relations with a woman." But since sexual immorality is occurring, each man should have sexual relations with his own wife, and each woman with her own husband. (1 Corinthians 7: 1–2)*
>
> *Marriage should be honored by all, and the marriage bed kept pure, for God will judge the adulterer and all the sexually immoral. (Hebrew 13:4)*

God considers all kinds of sex as a sin; it is only allowed under the covenant of marriage. So, if we are living together unmarried, then we are living in direct disobedience to the will of God. Heterosexual couples are guilty of fornication, while homosexual couples are guilty of fornication as well as the abomination of the same-sex relationship. Man may have made same-sex marriage legal in the eyes of the law, but it is judged the same by the word of God. God will never change. He is the same yesterday, today, and forever. Do not fall into Satan's trap of believing that what the world says is right or true without searching the word of God for yourself first. It has always been said, *"Then you will know the truth, and the truth will set you free" (John 8:32)*.

Oddly enough, when we get married after living together, things seem to change for the worst. We argue over every little thing and cannot manage to agree on anything. Then, factor in a few kids and life starts to take a rather hostile turn for the worst. As time goes on, we may stop and wonder just what went wrong. The fact is that, nothing went wrong with us. The problem started when we upset

Satan's plan by getting married and made a lifelong covenant with God to serve him and each other as one flesh. He wants us to continue to live in sin and out of the will of God, so our blessings and our prayers for ourselves and others will become ineffective.

Satan knows that we cannot serve two masters at the same time, because we will have to love one and hate the other. This is why we must choose our path wisely as to where we wish to go in our spiritual walk.

> *No one can serve two masters. Either you will hate*
> *the one and love the other, or you will be devoted to*
> *the one and despise the other. (Matthew 6:24)*

When two Christians get married, they form a union with more spiritual power than they would have individually. When the two pray and agree on any one thing, this kind of request to God carries more weight because it is coming from two hearts on one accord. This is why we should never marry someone who is an unbeliever or serves a different god and does not recognize Jesus Christ as his son. This situation of being unequally yoked, will cause us to never be on the same page spiritually, which is a battle we may spent a lifetime fighting and never win.

> *Do not be yoked together with unbelievers. For what*
> *do righteousness and wickedness have in common?*
> *Or what fellowship can light have with darkness?*
> *(2 Corinthians 6:14)*

When Christian couples are equally yoked spiritually and they have children, the children will be raised to be Christians, and the devil hates the thought of that ever happening. It is for this reason that the devil hates Christian couples and their children and wants to do everything he can to destroy them mentally, physically, and foremost spiritually. He knows that a Christian child will eventually grow up into a mature Christian adult who will possibly have children and raise them as they were raised, which is to service God, knowing we cannot have but one master.

Satan's only purpose is to win as many souls that he can before his time comes to an end, so he spends every waking moment trying to achieve this goal. This is why he hates the institution of marriage, because it was designed by God to populate the earth, and then our seeds will spread the gospel all over the world.

In order for us to be successful in marriage, we must first do it God's way and obey the rules of this covenant agreement. This is to love and honor God first and then, in like manner, do the same toward each other.

> **Wives, submit yourselves to your husbands,** *as is fitting in the Lord.* **Husbands, love your wives and do not be harsh with them.** *(Colossians 3:18–19)*
> *The wife does not have authority over her own body but yields it to her husband. In the same way, the husband does not have authority over his own body but yields it to his wife. (1 Corinthians 7:4)*

Wives should submit themselves to the authority of their *godly* husbands. If he is not saved, then this rule is not valid. A man must first be under God's authority before he has authority over his wife. If she is the only one who is serving God in the household, then her prayers are still effective but lack the power of a couple who is equally yoked in their faith. Also, men must love their wives as Christ loved the church, which means that we are willing to sacrifice all for her and the family. This is really what we signed up for when we said, "I do."

Second, we must adhere to God's rules on how to raise, care for, and discipline our children. We should teach them the gospel, provide for all their needs, spare not the rod, fulfill all of their godly desires, leave them with an inheritance for their future, and show them how to love God and their neighbor as themselves.

If we can manage to do all these things, we will soon discover that God will bless our marriage with a peace that will surpass all our earthly understanding. We will no longer have to suffer the tension that comes from not being on one accord with our spouse but experience the joy that only God can give with our lifelong companion.

When I finished college and returned home to live with my parents, I realized that I was still a dependent young adult. Shortly thereafter, I started my first job and got a place of my own. Now, I was my own man and completely independent to live as I pleased and, unfortunately, I did.

Years later, after I got married, I realized that I was no longer an independent person; I was back in the same situation that I was with my parents, in that they had say-so into what I could and could not do. I once again had to state where I was going, how long I would be gone, how much money I will spend, and what household duties I should perform. It was then that I realized that God meant for me to be raised and guided by him forever, and the only way that he can be assured of this coming to pass is to send me a godly, spirit-filled, lifelong spouse, who will love and correct me when I am wrong, praise me when I am right, and pray for me daily.

The reason for the friction in our marriage is to polish all the rough edges in our life until we can become close to being the perfect jewel that God created us to be. So, don't fight the system, just go with the flow and let God turn us into one of his masterpieces for all the world to see, and then, our life will shine and glorify him.

Remember, in order to have a healthy spiritual life in marriage, we must first love God, then our husband or wife, and then service our family and mankind with our time, talents, and resources. By doing this, the blessings from heaven will flow down to us and our family, along with God's favor and protection.

A Prayer for Marriage

Dear heavenly father, I ask, through all of your infinite grace and mercy that you continue to bless our marriage. Help us to love one another as you loved us, by showing us how to always put the other before ourselves. Continue to guard our hearts and mind from worldly people and vices that would come between us. If we are blessed with children, teach us how to raise them to be a blessing to you and the world. Also, Lord, let us not forsake our parents who raised us and help us to care for them in their later years so that they will have comfort and peace. We promise to serve you and one another until our earthly lives come to an end with you. We give you all the honor, all the glory, and all the praise. In the name of your son Jesus Christ, we pray. Amen.

Prayer for a Happy Marriage

Heavenly father, you are the one who has ordained marriage and who all marriages are made. You have always desired that your children find true happiness in the bonds of wedlock. Our prayer today is for genuine and true warmth and happiness in our marriage and in our home. Grant that our children may honor and glorify you. Teach us all how to live together within the confines of our home. Lead us in such a way that there will be no distrust one of the other, no acts of shame to hide from the world, and no show of impatience that will mar the beauty of our love and devotion. In it all, help us to do your will in everything. We ask it in the name of your son Jesus Christ. Amen.

Key Scriptures

Please read the entire chapter of each verse for greater edification and understanding.

1. *Leviticus 18:22*
2. *Genesis 2:18, 21–24*
3. *1 Corinthians 7: 1–2*
4. *Hebrew 13:4*
5. *John 8:32*
6. *Matthew 6:24*
7. *2 Corinthians 6:14*
8. *Colossians 3:18–19*
9. *1 Corinthians 7: 4*

CHAPTER SIX

Discovering God's Spirit of Victory through Faith and Self-Control

I can do all this through him who gives me strength.
(Philippians 4:13)

What one thing can cause us to succeed or fail, love or hate, reach physical maturity or stagnate our mental growth, and finally grow spiritually or fall into worldly despair? We face this adversary that can destroy our future, kill our dreams, darken our hopes, weaken our faith and blind us to real truth. This thing that we face every day is our self.

The definition of self-control is the ability to control oneself, in particular one's emotions, desires, and/or their expression toward one's behavior, especially in difficult situations. Other words that are synonymous with self-control are self-discipline, self-restraint, self-possession, self-command, willpower, composure, coolness, moderation, temperance and abstemious. Many of these parallel the fruit of the spirit.

The person we see in the mirror can be our best friend or our worst enemy. How many times have we seen individuals with great potential and knew that they possessed the ability to achieve anything they put their minds to. At the same time, they fail to realize the same God-given greatness in themselves. We read self-motivational books, attend workshops and seminars on the power of positive thinking and pay enormous fees for counseling, psychologists and psychiatrists. We watch and listen to a wide variety of inspirational videos and CDs. We are willing to do all of these things simply because we cannot manage to have enough faith in the word of God to have faith in ourselves. As we strengthen our faith in God, it will increase the faith we have in ourselves. We need to master self-control.

For we live by faith, not by sight. (2 Corinthians 5:7)

We must grow and mature to the point that we no longer depend on our physical vision but on the spiritual vision given to us from God.

Consequently, faith comes from hearing the message, and the message is heard through the word of Christ. (Romans 10:17)

Yes, the word of God, along with the God-inspired teachings of Jesus Christ, is the main source of our faith. We can use this faith to defeat this demonic spirit of self-doubt, which drives us to self-destruction. By using godly self-control, we can reach our destiny and fulfill our dreams of success and happiness.

Now faith is confidence in what we hope for and assurance about what we do not see. (Hebrews 11:1)

Every Sunday morning, when I was young, I would look forward to reading the comics. My favorite one was Peanuts. Charlie Brown, the main character, was depicted as someone who always lets life rain on his parade. He was constantly worrying about everything, and he was usually the butt of all the jokes. Although considerate, friendly, and polite to everyone, he is considered to be a blockhead and a loser to his friends as well as to himself.

Charlie Brown failed at everything that he tried to accomplish. The one thing that sticks out in my mind is the annual football kickoff with his so-called friend Lucy, who would hold the ball for him. Every time, Lucy would talk him into kicking this football by feeding his ego and telling him, "This time, we can do it, Charlie Brown." But every time, she would pull that ball away at the last second and watch with joy as poor Charlie Brown went flying through the air, landing flat on his back. Charlie Brown desired to complete this task so badly that he would trust Lucy over and over again, only to receive the same painful results. He lived a life of suffering, which was not only due to the ill will of so-called friend Lucy but rather because he had no faith in himself and possessed a defeated spirit.

Faith and self-control could have saved Charlie Brown years of heartache and pain, because a God-centered mindset would have helped him make wise decisions. The pain of the past would have taught him to not trust Lucy and get someone more trustworthy to hold the ball or maybe find another sport to achieve victory. He could then apply this wisdom of self-control to other aspects of his life. If we control our thoughts and actions, then it will directly affect our destiny.

A lot of us are walking around with a defeated spirit just like old Charlie Brown, which keeps us from fulfilling our God-given destiny. We believe we've failed before we start the task. We quit in the first half of the game. We wave the white flag before the first shot is fired. When we do these things, we truly offend God, because he is a God of victory, and defeat is not in his vocabulary.

Every now and then, we will see a game where a team is really behind in the first half but come back to win in the second. The head coach, at half time, preached to them about faith and the power of self-control, and as a collective group; they were able to overcome the odds against them. This is why we must practice feeding the spirit with the word of God as often as we can because without his word in our hearts to build us up, we will fall for anything and fail at everything. This is the difference between God's spirit of victory and the devil's spirit of defeat. Let us go forth from this moment on with a positive mind as well as a strong faith in God and ourselves. Once we have these things in place in our lives, we cannot fail.

We cannot afford to continue living with self-doubt because it causes us to fall into the world's trap set by Satan. His job is to fill our minds with negative images about ourselves and others. These negative thoughts give birth to negative actions, which ultimately leads way to negative results or consequences. All that is good, perfect, and positive is of God, and everything that is bad, imperfect, and negative is of Satan.

What kind of results do we want in our lives? If we follow God's word, the wisdom and teachings of Jesus Christ and have a strong faith, we will conquer the demon of self-destruction and become the good and faithful servant that God created us to be. When we decided to serve God, he will see to it that we succeed far above our own limited expectations.

> *Now to him who is able to do immeasurably more*
> *than all we ask or imagine, according to his power*
> *that is at work within us. (Ephesians 3:20)*

God expects us to give him praise, honor, and public recognition for his divine role in our success. He requires it because this will be the way we can let the world know who helped us get the victory. So, give credit where credit is due.

Do not become your own worst enemy. Through God's infinite wisdom, we can eliminate the fear of failure and replace it with the faith of a winner. We do not need to look for others to build us up or fall short of our goal because we allowed others to tear us down. Instead, we should build up our faith to the point that nothing is impossible.

> *Truly I tell you, if anyone says to this mountain,*
> *'Go, throw yourself into the sea,' and does not doubt*
> *in their heart but believes that what they say will*
> *happen, it will be done for them. (Mark 11:23)*

We live in evil days, but that does not mean that the evil has to live in us. The spiritual sickness in today's society was designed to keep us in a constant state of fear, doubt, and depression. Godly faith and self-control will keep us free from the pitfalls of worldly vices, such as, addictions to money, sex, drugs, alcohol, and power. All of these things were designed by Satan to give us a false sense of peace. But true peace can only come from the Lord.

> *It teaches us to say No to ungodliness and worldly passions, and to live self-controlled, upright and godly lives in this present age. (Titus 2:12)*

A free spirit is a healthy spirit, because it is based on the word of God, which is the truth. We must take control of our lives by letting his word control our heart. Once God has control of our heart, then we will be in perfect spiritual health and have a peace that surpasses all worldly understanding.

> *And the peace of God, which transcends all under- standing, will guard your hearts and minds in Christ Jesus. (Philippians 4:7)*

Prayer for the Spirit of Victory

Lord, God, most gracious heavenly father, who has sustained me from the moment of my creation and continues to pour mercy and grace over me now. I thank you for designing me with a divine destiny and purpose and for equipping me with necessary talents for this task, along with the power of your holy word to guide me in the right direction. I trust you to guard my mind, heart, and spirit, that I will not fall prey to the enemies' traps of self-doubt and confusion concerning my purpose. You said no weapon formed against me shall prosper or succeed in stopping me from fulfilling the destiny that you created me for. You said that I am more than a conqueror, so I claim victory in every situation that I face with you by my side. Help me to remove self-doubt from every area of my life so that my actions will always be a reflection of your grace. I ask these things in the loving name of your son Jesus Christ. Amen.

Key Scriptures

Please read the entire chapter of each verse for greater edification and understanding.

1. *Philippians 4:13*
2. *2 Corinthians 5:7*
3. *Romans 10:17*
4. *Hebrews 11:1*
5. *Ephesians 3:20*
6. *Mark 11:23*
7. *Titus 2:12*
8. *Philippians 4:7*

CHAPTER SEVEN

Faith and Love
The Key Ingredients to God's
Grace and Mercy

*And without faith it is impossible to please God,
because anyone who comes to him must believe that
he exists and that he rewards those who earnestly
seek him. (Hebrews 11:6)*

Faith and love are the two most important ingredients in our spiritual and physical lives. They are the substances that make our relationship with God complete. Without these two elements, the recipe for salvation and eternal life would cease to exist, because it takes both to be a born-again believer.

*Now faith is confidence in what we hope for and
assurance about what we do not see. (Hebrews 11:1)*

This is God's definition of faith, which is the main factor of the relationship we have with him. We need to continually study his word in order to strengthen our faith and, in turn, build a stronger and closer relationship with him. The greater our faith, the more we please him. This will allow him to bless us more abundantly.

Jesus replied: "Love the Lord your God with all your heart and with all your soul and with all your mind." (Matthew 22:37)

Charity is love, which is the foundation of our faith. We build upon it with the word of God when we live by showing love for one another. God's love for us strengthens this spiritual foundation, which makes it solid and unmovable. With total love for and faith in God and his son Jesus, our lives are made whole. We must understand that these are two key ingredients in this recipe of life. Strong faith in and an endless love for God are the things that are required to start growing in God's grace and receiving his divine mercy. This also insures us that God's hedge of protection will be around us and our family always.

In 2004, Mel Gibson, a famous movie actor, director, and film producer, decided to make a movie about the last days in the life of Jesus Christ, titled *The Passion of Christ*. This movie was painful for me to watch because of the love that I have for my Lord and savior Jesus Christ. It was as if I were watching a close family member and friend being tortured to death, along with the feeling of helplessness in not being able to do anything about it. The images in this movie are something that I will never forget! The pain and suffering of Jesus is truly hard to read about and even more difficult to watch on the big screen. To this day, I still have a hard time watching this movie and seeing the cruel and inhumane treatment of Jesus, whose only crime was loving us.

The Hollywood movie critics said that the movie was too violent, even though the word of God states the events to be accurate accounts of the Jews and Roman governments' actions during the crucifixion. The Jewish leaders said the movie made them look evil, but the Bible states that they were the ones who called for the crucifixion to take place. So, the movie went from being a Christian film about Jesus' suffering for our sins to an extremely violent, anti-Semitic statement of one group's perception of his death.

You may be wondering why I choose to speak of this in a chapter on faith and love. Well, this is because I realized that *The Passion of Christ* was not an overviolent, anti-Semitic movie, but rather a *love story*. This love story spoke of God's great love for us, where he offered the life of his only begotten son to brutally die for our sins. This movie also showed how much faith and love it took for Jesus to allow himself to be subjected to this kind of torture, in order to fulfill the will of the Father. In my personal option, this was the greatest love story of all times.

> *For God so loved the world that he gave his one and only Son, that whoever believes in him shall not perish but have eternal life. (John 3:16)*

The famous pastor and civil rights leader, Rev. Dr. Martin Luther King, Jr., who was assassinated in Memphis, Tennessee, on April 4, 1968, made the profound statement that "If any man has not found anything that he is willing to *die* for, then he is not fit to *live*." Dr. King was a man truly led by the word and spirit of God, because this statement is one he lived by and died believing. This spoke of the level of faith and love he possessed for God, Jesus, and the Holy Spirit as well as for his fellowman. He knew the true meaning of love and faith and the sacrifice that would be required to fulfill his dream and God-given destiny.

In order to be truly spiritually healthy, we need to follow the example of those in our past who have shown us the way. We need to study the word of God more intensely to receive the necessary understanding of his gospel so that we can have the power we need to be the Christian soldiers that He can use in this earthly spiritual battle.

> *Do your best to present yourself to God as one approved, a worker who does not need to be ashamed and who correctly handles the word of truth. (2 Timothy 2:15)*
>
> *For our struggle is not against flesh and blood, but against the rulers, against the authorities, against the powers of this dark world and against*

the spiritual forces of evil in the heavenly realms.
(Ephesians 6:12)

Once we realize just who God is, then we can start to visualize the awesome power that *he* has blessed us with, enabling us to live in the daily presence of sin. We must learn to trust God to answer our prayers, solve our problems, heal our bodies, increase our finances, and give us peace in our home and joy in our hearts. Remember that God loves us, and our faith and love for him and others are all that *he* requires of us to receive his mercy and grace.

> *In fact, this is love for God: to keep his commands.*
> *And his commands are not burdensome, for every-*
> *one born of God overcomes the world. This is the*
> *victory that has overcome the world, even our faith.*
> *Who is it that overcomes the world? Only*
> *the one who believes that Jesus is the Son of God.*
> *(1 John 5:3–5)*

We live in a sin-sick world. Every day, we watch the news and witness the inhuman acts of men and lack of love for one another. Mass shootings, domestic violence, internet bullying, identity theft, child abuse, and animal cruelty are all on the rise worldwide. The forum of public opinion will make a weak attempt to find worldly answers to this spiritual problem, but no solutions will be found. God stated that all these things would come to pass in the last days, as stated in the last book of the bible titled Revelations. If we read it, then the present world conditions would not be a surprise but exactly what's to be expected. However, a spiritually healthy person will fair very well in these troubling times because the mercy and grace of God will be upon them and a hedge of protection around them.

Do not become a victim of these times, but be the one who will be there to help rescue others by showing them a better and safer path to take by having total faith in God. Refuse to be a part of the problem by being a part of the solution. As we continue to grow in faith in God and love for one another, we can make this world a spiritually healthier place to live.

Prayer of Faith

Heavenly father, make us strong in you so that we may stand fast in our faith, and help us to go forward today remembering that you promised to be with us always. Teach us how to love one another as you have loved us. Show us how to forgive others as you have forgiven us time after time. You truly love and trust us, because you are so faithful and loving to us, even when we truly do not deserve it. Thank you for your son Jesus, who showed his love for us by his sacrifice on the cross for our sins. Never remove your hedge of protection from us so that we may stay shielded from the sins of this world. In the mighty name Jesus Christ, we pray. Amen.

Key Scriptures

Please read the entire chapter of each verse for greater edification and understanding.

1. *Hebrews 11:6*
2. *Hebrews 11:1*
3. *Matthew 22:37*
4. *John 3:16*
5. *2 Timothy 2:15*
6. *Ephesians 6:15*
7. *1 John 5:3–5*

CHAPTER EIGHT

Growing in Grace

When I was a child, I talked like a child, I thought like a child, I reasoned like a child. When I became a man, I put the ways of childhood behind me. (1 Corinthians 13:11)

Growing up can be a very difficult process, especially during the transitional period from being a teenager to becoming an adult. We must go about our lives differently by taking on different responsibilities as we grow and mature. Along with these responsibilities comes a task that can wear us down if we lack the mental maturity as well as the sincere faith in God to handle them. Without a stable mind and a strong faith, we would find ourselves falling prey to the world's system for all the answers to our problems. All this time, we have not realized that the same world-based system that we look to for solutions is the same system that is responsible for creating the problems we are trying to solve.

For example: Would we, while competing in a sporting event, go to our opponent for information on how to win the game? Then, why would we think that the world can give us answers to a problem it has created to defeat us physically and destroy our spirit? There is no logic in this strategy to victory, because the system is one that was designed for our failure, and God's system is made for our victory. We need to stop depending on the world to solve worldly problems, but we must rather depend on the world's creator and savior to guide us to a new way of thinking. God's wisdom will give us answers to that which we seek.

> *So I say to you: Ask and it will be given to you; seek and you will find; knock and the door will be opened to you. For everyone who asks receives; the one who seeks finds; and to the one who knocks, the door will be opened. (Luke 11:9–10)*

This may sound easy, but it is not. The reason that we have to not only grow up physically but also spiritually is to reach the level of faith and maturity which supplies the wisdom needed to solve our earthly problems.

> *Get wisdom, get understanding; do not forget my words or turn away from them. (Proverbs 4:5)*

In order to get a better understanding of spiritual growth, we can first cover a process of which we have firsthand knowledge, and that is the progression of our growth physically.

First, at birth, we are babies who are totally dependent on our parents and others for our every need, hope, and desire. Without their loving care, we would not survive.

Second, we progress into the toddler stage. Although still dependent on our parents and others for everything, we start learning some of the ways of our caregivers through observation and experimentation. Since we have become more mobile, the knowledge we receive, concerning right and wrong, is needed for our safety. However, the need for others' care is still essential to our survival.

The third stage of our developmental process deals with the young child, preteen, and teenager years. These three phases start to reveal the gradual loss of dependency we have on our caregivers, which is directly linked to an increased wisdom and knowledge of our worldly environment. While we are not totally free to take on the world alone, we possess a great deal of information that will prepare us when the need arises.

Finally, there are the phases called the young adult, adult, and senior citizen, which will carry us into the final phase known as the golden years. In these final stages, we should be totally independent from our caregivers. We should have all the necessary wisdom that we need to make our way in this world as well as the means to provide for our self and other family members.

In viewing the process of spiritual growth in a similar fashion, we find that the process of maturing in our spiritual life is paramount to serving God totally. If we never grow up spiritually, then we will never develop an independent faith. This is the type of faith that does not require men's encouragement to do the right things, but the kind that guides us through life with God's word.

When we are spiritual infants, our pastor, their staff, and hopefully our parents and friends act as our spiritual guardians to nurture us until we can walk in the ways of the Lord on our own. We will require the assistance and support of fellow Christians as they are our extended family.

Once we reach the toddler stage of our spiritual growth and we begin to learn more of God's word, then it will enable us to walk more by faith. The pastor and staff will still play a vital role in our spiritual growth, but through observation, listening, and being obedient to God's word, we will grow stronger and become more confident in facing the world's daily situations.

The third stage of growing in our faith comes when we start to seek God's word on our own. This is the time we spend studying the Bible aside from our weekly worship service or Bible study. This is the one-on-one time we spend with God. It is often referred to as our intimate time with the master. This is the sign of a truly mature Christian, because we do not need to be forced-fed with his daily bread, but we rather have a hunger for his holy wisdom on our own. Finally, after we have gained godly wisdom, knowledge and understanding, we will be mature enough to teach others by witnessing to them as God gives us utterance (review "*Opening the Door to Salvation*").

> *But it is the spirit in a person, the breath of the*
> *Almighty, that gives them understanding. (Job 32:8)*

Spiritual growth and maturity are extremely important for our overall success in life. The daily trials and tribulations that we face will easily overcome a childish spirit, because we have not matured enough in God's knowledge and wisdom to discern good from evil. The reason is that if we do not know God's word, we will not be able to recognize his voice when we are living outside of his holy will and living an ungodly lifestyle.

> *My people are destroyed from lack of knowledge.*
> *"Because you have rejected knowledge, I also reject*
> *you as my priests; because you have ignored the*
> *law of your God, I also will ignore your children.*
> *(Hosea 4:6)*

A Christian can be a spiritual baby at any age, and some never fully mature. This is mainly due to the fact that we refuse to grow up and never take the time to find a good church home that will help us to mature in our faith. It has to be one that will feed our spirit the type of knowledge that we will need to survive in this world (refer to chapter nine on finding the right church for you to grow).

The Restaurant Theory: The Quality of Spiritual Food

When we go out to eat, we select a restaurant that serves food that is pleasing to our taste, offers great service and at a reasonable price. This is a place we would gladly tell our family and friends about, because we always leave full and satisfied. Likewise, the house of God is a spiritual restaurant that feeds the spirit–man so that we will become full and satisfied with his word, and it will help guide us through life's daily challenges until we return to dine again.

Jesus answered, "It is written: 'Man shall not live on bread alone.'" (Luke 4:4)

The place where we feed our spirit must be able to nourish our heart, mind, and soul to the point that we actually feel spiritually full. If our church cannot produce this godly feeling of spiritual satisfaction, then we need to find another place to receive our daily bread. Some people feel that it is not necessary to go to church to please God. They think that they can stay at home, listen to a TV or radio sermon, play a cassette, CD, or DVD, or just play a little Christian music in the car or around the house. The fact is that God requires our presence with the sacrifice of our time, talent and financial resources, as well as, the public showing of praise from our mouth. This lets him know that we love him and we are not ashamed to let the world know how we feel about him. It is understood that everyone cannot be at the church that they feel connected to for their spiritual diet because of distance or a job. In this case, make sure you are consistent in your worship time and giving to that ministry through tithes and offerings.

Growing in grace is very important in our Christian lives. However, we need to understand just what God's grace really is. The following is a bit of history that, hopefully, will aid in our understanding of this gift from the master.

Captain John Newton, whose father taught him how to sail at the young age of eleven, became a slave ship operator at twenty-two. On May 10, 1748, he was trapped in a violent storm at sea. He had never witnessed anything this frightening before, and now he feared for his life, his crew as well as the cargo full of African slaves. It was with this feeling of helplessness that he prayed, "Lord, have mercy upon us and deliver us safely from this deadly situation." He prayed that upon his survival, he would give his life in total service to God.

For the rest of his life, Captain John Newton would observe May 10 as the anniversary of his day of conversion and the renewing of his faith in God. The storm was a day of humiliation in which he had to subject his will to a much higher power, which is the will of God. He wrote these words of his experience, *"Thro' many dangers, toils, and snares, I have already come; 'tis grace has bro't me safe thus far, and grace will lead me home."* These words, anointed by God, would become one of the most popular and prophetic hymns of all time. The song is "Amazing Grace" and here are the words to the famous first verse.

> Amazing grace how sweet the sound
> That saved a wretch like me.
> I once was lost, but now I'm found,
> Was blind, but now I see.
> 'Twas grace that taught my heart to fear,
> And grace my fears relieved.
> How precious did that grace appear
> The hour I first believed. (Amazing Grace by
> Captain John Newton)

This hymn, which has been performed by millions all over the world, tells the story of what God's grace can do if we truly believe and trust him. I have heard this hymn, which has been performed many times, in many different ways, but it was not until recently that I realized what the author was truly saying about grace.

Captain Newton stated that grace was a sweet sound that saved him. It was this statement that made me realize that grace is a sound, which is the voice of God that comes in the form of his holy word. The holy Bible is his written word, and Jesus Christ is the living word that lives in us by way of the Holy Spirit. These three elements are the key to receiving this saving grace.

The next time we find ourselves in the mist of one of life's storms, we need only to go to the word of God for deliverance. He promised us that he would never leave us nor forsake us. Let's not go down with the ship, but instead, let us overcome our worldly circumstances with his amazing grace.

Grace is a key element of our spiritual health. It is necessary for the healing from all the problems that will arise in our daily lives. It is like a divine insurance policy on our soul, with a premium paid with our obedience to his word, praise for his blessing, and love for him and our neighbor. Don't let this spiritual policy lapse and leave you and your family totally unprotected, because it can be fatal.

> *No one will be able to stand against you all the days of your life. As I was with Moses, so I will be with you; I will never leave you nor forsake you. (Joshua 1:5)*

A Prayer for Grace

O Lord, our God, we pray that our lives may be free from sin and a testimony to your wonderful saving power and grace. Help us to grow spiritually each and every day in a way that will be pleasing to you and of benefit to your kingdom. Teach us how to exercise our faith and become stronger Christians so that as we grow in your grace, we increase in faith also. In Jesus' mighty name, we pray. Amen.

Key Scriptures

Please read the entire chapter of each verse for greater edification and understanding.

1. *1 Corinthians 13:11*
2. *Luke 11:9–10*
3. *Proverbs 4:5*
4. *Job 32:8*
5. *Hosea 4:6*
6. *Luke 4:4*
7. *Joshua 1:5*

CHAPTER NINE

A Good Shepherd

I will place shepherds over them who will tend them,
and they will no longer be afraid or terrified, nor will
any be missing," declares the Lord. (Jeremiah 23:4)

The world is full of shepherds. They are tending to their flocks, helping them to find food that will nourish their bodies and give them strength for the journey. They lead them to cool, refreshing streams to quench their thirst, and in the still of the night, they stand guard to ward off the enemies that try to devour them. A good shepherd is the key to the survival of the flock.

It is the inherited nature of sheep to live in herds, because they do not know how to lead or protect themselves. They always require the guidance of someone outside of the flock to get them to their final destination. This is why God created the shepherd, so they could guide, protect, and care for his flock. However, a bad shepherd who does not tend to his flock properly will allow them to become lost in the wilderness, unable to find food or water, and eventually die or get devoured by predators. If the shepherd fails to protect the flock, he will suffer reproach from the flocks' owner, and according to the word of God, their fate will be worse than that of those lost from the herd.

Woe to the worthless shepherd, who deserts the flock!
May the sword strike his arm and his right eye! May

his arm be completely withered, his right eye totally blinded! (Zechariah 11:17)

We, who are born-again believers are the flock who graze in the pastures of God's blessing. The shepherds are the men and women who he has ordained to lead his flock to the promise land of eternal life with him and Jesus Christ. Unfortunately, we find that all shepherds are not appointed or anointed by him, and the sheep are the ones who will ultimately suffer. A bad shepherd who is not willing to take the time to learn from the wisdom of God and his son Jesus, the master shepherd, will never know what the flock truly needs and how to teach them to protect themselves from all the enemies of this world and avoid dangerous situations.

My people have been lost sheep; their shepherds have led them astray and caused them to roam on the mountains. They wandered over mountain and hill and forgot their own resting place. (Jeremiah 50:6)

Shepherding is one of the most important positions in the development of a Christian's religious life, and they are in drastic need of spiritual first aid to fulfill their duties. The failure of a good shepherd to effectively teach God's word leads their flock into dangerous areas that can cause them to become spiritually hungry, lost, and wounded. Hungry for the true word needed to fill them, lost to God's holy will to guide them, and left to suffer spiritually at the hands of Satan's world system, which is designed to destroy them.

Good shepherds are the priests, pastors, evangelists, apostles, and leaders of the church who study to show themselves approved by God to fulfill this task. However, all of those who claim to be called into the ministry by God have not been chosen to do so. For this reason, we have false shepherds, leading flocks all around the world to a certain spiritual death.

Watch out for false prophets. They come to you in sheep's clothing, but inwardly they are ferocious wolves. (Matthew 7:15)

Our spiritual guidance is the key factor to our spiritual health. If our shepherd is lost spiritually, then it will be impossible for them to lead us into the promises of God. This is why it is extremely important to choose the right shepherd for you and your family.

Jesus Christ is the greatest shepherd who has ever walked the face of the earth. He loved his flock so much that he died for them. He kept them spiritually healthy by feeding them the true word of God and practicing the things that he preached. He protected them from the evil of this world with his faith and Godly wisdom.

I am the good shepherd; I know my sheep and my sheep know me—just as the Father knows me and I know the Father—and I lay down my life for the sheep. I have other sheep that are not of this sheep pen. I must bring them also. They too will listen to my voice, and there shall be one flock and one shepherd. (John 10:14–16)

Who is your shepherd? Do they lead you with utmost concern for your spiritual health like Jesus did? Are they truly led by the spirit of God in what they say, what they do, and where they go? Do they feed your spirit until you are full and satisfied?

If the answer to any of these questions is "no," then why are we still grazing in their barren pasture? In the real world, a shepherd is given a flock to lead, and the sheep have no say so in the matter. However, in the spiritual world, we choose the shepherd who will guide us, and it is very important that we find one using godly wisdom and a discerning spirit.

There was another great shepherd who had a heart for God and tremendous love for his flock, and his name was King David, born in 1040 BCE, the eighth and youngest son of Jesse and Nitzevet of

Bethlehem. His father trained him to be a shepherd, and he performed the job with great honor and courage.

David, while still in his youth, killed a lion and a bear to protect his flock. The details of these encounters were explained to King Saul, in *1 Samuel 17:33–36*. The King was looking for someone to defeat the Philistine giant Goliath. God sent David because he knew he had the faith and courage needed to deal with Goliath, who spoke so disrespectfully against his God and the children of Israel.

David used the same weapon that he used against the lion and the bear, a slingshot and stones, to defeat Goliath the Philistine giant. As a result of this great victory, he was appointed to be the court musician and armor bearer for Israel's first king Saul.

David, as a young man, used the training from his earthly father to be a good shepherd, but later guided by God, his heavenly father, he became a great one. He loved God with a passion few could match, and he decided early in his life that the God he served and the flock he protected were both worth dying for.

The godly experience he received from the encounter with the lion and the bear were just what he needed to prepare him for the battle with the Goliath. The favor he received from God, for killing Goliath, was exactly what he needed to lead his new flock, which was the nation of Israel and the Philistines who agreed to serve him upon the death of their leader, Goliath. Due to his love and devotion to his flocks of the past, God decided to give David a new flock to lead. With his divine shepherding experience, it made him the right man for the job, because of his love and devotion to this flock. These are the qualities we need to look for in a good shepherd.

As we study the life of King David, we realize that he was a good shepherd but not a perfect man. No shepherd is going to be perfect, but they should study and follow the word of God. In order to know if they are correct in their teachings, we must know the holy word for ourselves, less we will be led astray.

If we are truly concerned about our spiritual health and that of our families, then we need to find a spirit-filled flock to worship with and a godly, Holy Spirit led shepherd to be our guide. Our church home is the place we go to feed on God's holy word. The duty of our shepherd lies in helping us receive divine inspiration, direction, and guidance to help us heal the spiritual wounds that the world inflects upon us along life's journey.

> *Then I will give you shepherds after my own heart, who will lead you with knowledge and understanding. (Jeremiah 3:15)*

I realized a long time ago that the three main shepherds in my life would be God, Jesus, and the Holy Spirit. In making this decision, I know that my soul is in good hands at all times. I also have a fourth shepherd, my pastor, who makes sure I am fed the true word of God. I have no doubt that my family and I are being well fed, divinely guided, and spiritually grounded in these evil days. We need to follow the words and wisdom of these great shepherds of our past and let God be the first good shepherd in our life. He will help us find the shepherd we need to show us the truth and the way and keep our spirits healthy and safe.

We must ask ourselves, who is our good shepherd?

> *The Lord is my shepherd, I lack nothing.*
>
> *He makes me lie down in green pastures, he leads me beside quiet waters, he refreshes my soul. He guides me along the right paths for his name's sake.*
>
> *Even though I walk through the darkest valley, I will fear no evil, for you are with me; your rod and your staff, they comfort me.*
>
> *You prepare a table before me in the presence of my enemies. You anoint my head with oil; my cup overflows.*
>
> *Surely your goodness and love will follow me all the days of my life, and I will dwell in the house of the Lord forever. (Psalms 23:1–6)*

Let us continue to use the life of Jesus Christ as the blueprint of a good shepherd and in keeping with the will of God, his father, died for the sins of his sheep.

Jesus knew the importance of following God's word and being obedient to his will as it related to the life of the flock. Jesus chose to live and die as an example for other shepherds to follow.

Jesus left us physically, but he left us with another spiritual shepherd to lead us called the Holy Spirit that directs us from the inside out. However, we cannot follow this guide if we are spiritually disconnected from the heavenly father. The health of our relationship with God is the light that we need to find the path to our destiny, and the shepherd is the one who makes sure we arrive safely. When we continue to stay within the will of the father and are obedient to his ways, then our spirit–man can avoid the curses that await us. Let's follow the right shepherd for our spiritual well-being and we will never hunger and thirst or become lost in the wilderness of worldly situations again.

A Prayer for a Good Shepherd

Lord God, our most gracious heavenly father, we thank you so much for sending your son Jesus Christ, as a living sacrifice, to die for all our sins. Now, as we look for a place to worship and learn your word, we ask that the Holy Spirit give us divine discernment to find a good shepherd in which to follow. Give them godly wisdom and knowledge to lead their flock in the right direction. Shield their heart and mind from worldly influences of evil. Continue to guide us with your word so we will know when our shepherd has turned away from their divine purpose, which will enable us to guard our souls from being lost. Thank you that we can use your son Jesus as an example to follow in our earthly quest in finding a good shepherd today. All this we ask in the holy name of Jesus Christ. Amen

Key Scriptures

Please read the entire chapter of each verse for greater edification and understanding.

1. *Jeremiah 23:4*
2. *Zechariah 11:17*
3. *Jeremiah 50:6*
4. *Matthew 7:15*
5. *John 10:14–16*
6. *Jeremiah 3:15*
7. *1 Samuel 17:33–36*
8. *Jeremiah 3:15*
9. *Psalms 23:1–6*

CHAPTER TEN

Fatal Attraction:
God Loves the Sinner
but Hates the Sin

The two angels arrived at Sodom in the evening, and Lot was sitting in the gateway of the city. When he saw them, he got up to meet them and bowed down with his face to the ground.

"My lords," he said, "please turn aside to your servant's house. You can wash your feet and spend the night and then go on your way early in the morning." "No," they answered, "we will spend the night in the square."

But he insisted so strongly that they did go with him and entered his house. He prepared a meal for them, baking bread without yeast, and they ate.

Before they had gone to bed, all the men from every part of the city of Sodom—both young and old—surrounded the house.

They called to Lot, "Where are the men who came to you tonight? Bring them out to us so that we can have sex with them."

Lot went outside to meet them and shut the door behind him and said, "No, my friends. Don't do this wicked thing.

Look, I have two daughters who have never slept with a man. Let me bring them out to you, and you can do what you like with them. But don't do anything to these men, for they have come under the protection of my roof."

"Get out of our way," they replied. "This fellow came here as a foreigner, and now he wants to play the judge! We'll treat you worse than them." They kept bringing pressure on Lot and moved forward to break down the door.

But the men inside reached out and pulled Lot back into the house and shut the door.

Then they struck the men who were at the door of the house, young and old, with blindness so that they could not find the door.

The two men said to Lot, "Do you have anyone else here—sons-in-law, sons or daughters, or anyone else in the city who belongs to you? Get them out of here, because we are going to destroy this place. The outcry to the Lord against its people is so great that he has sent us to destroy it." (Genesis 19:1–13)

The story of Sodom and Gomorra was about a place where breaking every commandment of God was a daily way of life. Even though this event was before God gave the ten commandments to Moses, man still knew right from wrong and there was not one thing sacred about this city. They loved living in complete disobedience to God's law, so to stop this spiritual disease from spreading to other lands, he decided to burn it to the ground, along with every man, woman, and child within its gates. This way, no one here could ever carry this culture of sinful corruption to other lands. God knows that the gay lifestyle will always be woven into the fabric of society, but he wants us to know without any doubt that he will never approve or accept it. He will always love the sinner but hate the sin.

The two angels had come to warn Lot and his family of God's plan to destroy the city due to their extreme sinful activities, sexual immorality, and ungodly beliefs. After informing Lot of God's plan, Lot begged them to leave, because he knew the evil that existed within its gates. While the angels refused to leave, a hostile crowd was trying to enter Lot's house by force, but the angels opened the door and caused the gang to go blind, which caused them to wonder aimlessly on the streets. They then told Lot to take his family out of the city, because it would soon be destroyed by fire.

> *Do not have sexual relations with a man as one does with a woman; that is detestable. (Leviticus 18:22)*

This area was one big orgy, with all manner of sin present. It was completely out of control spiritually and physically, because there were no righteous people living in this dark city to show them the light.

The question is not "Did God hate this lifestyle then" but rather, "Does He feel the same way today?" The answer is "yes, he does," because God and his word will never change. So, if we call ourselves God-fearing, Christian people, then why are we accepting it with open arms and allowing it to become such a big part of our daily lives and calling it normal?

> *Jesus Christ is the same yesterday and today and forever. (Hebrews 13:8)*

Since God, Jesus Christ, and the Holy Spirit are one entity, then this stands to prove that their opinion on the matter of homosexuality should be very clear. The point is that homosexual behavior was not, is not, and never will be acceptable in their eyes. So why is it becoming so acceptable in ours?

Lot, who was a part of the blessed seed of Abraham through his son Isaac, decided to leave the other tribes and move to this region of Sodom and Gomorrah. This region was extremely sinful in the eyes of God, because they did not follow any of his teaching or laws. His uncle Abraham was the one God had chosen as the father of all nations. His seed would be raised to follow the teachings of God and spread this message across the land. This godly connection is what kept Lot and his family safe from God's judgment of the city.

> *Against all hope, Abraham in hope believed and so became the father of many nations, just as it had been said to him, "So shall your offspring be."* (Romans 4:18)

The true role of a father is to provide, protect, counsel, and correct his children. If the child is obedient to the father's rules, then they are rewarded with things above and beyond their daily needs. However, when they disobey his rules, there will be consequences. These may be physical punishment, the loss of privileges, or the cutting off of funds. If there is no disadvantage connected to the disobedient behavior, then there would be no reason to do that which is right. When a father raises his children with godly direction, then they will grow up to be a blessing to the world. God is our heavenly father, and he is trying to teach us to follow his ways, which will make the world a better place to live, but if we are disobedient to his rules, then there will always be a price we have to pay.

Let's take a moment to understand his uncle, Abraham, the father of many nations. Abraham had to first show God that he had enough faith to carry out this task, so God told him to go up into the mountains and sacrifice his only son Isaac, as a burnt offering unto him. Isaac was the son that God promised to give to him and his wife Sarah. The miracle of Isaac's conception is the fact that Abraham was ninety-nine years old and Sarah, whose womb was already dry and unable to bear children, was around the age of ninety.

> *By faith Abraham, when God tested him, offered Isaac as a sacrifice. He who had embraced the promises was about to sacrifice his one and only son, 18 even though God had said to him, "It is through Isaac that your offspring will be reckoned."* (Hebrews 11:17–18)

If we look closely at this Scripture, we see the promises of God. First, he said to Abraham and Sarah, "I will give you a son." Next, he stated, "You and this child will be the father of many nations." Abraham's faith allowed him to go along with God's wishes, because he knew that something had to happen at the sacrificial altar for God's promise to come to pass and for his son to be the father of generations to come.

God then told Abraham to use his son as a living sacrifice unto him, so he trusted God and followed his instructions. Just before he was about to kill Isaac, an angel told him to stop and not harm the child, then a ram appeared in the bush to serve as the sacrifice. God's word is so absolute that stopping Abraham was planned and so was the appearance of the ram, because a sacrifice had to be made if that is what was promised. God's word never changes.

In today's society, the world has become more accepting of the homosexual lifestyle and, to a greater degree, more understanding of the nature of the emotions that grow from it. The world's prospective of the gay lifestyle has changed to that of a greater worldwide acceptance, but not God's. His view will never change, and the consequences of a same-sex relationship, which is that of an abominable sin, will forever be the same.

It has to be understood that God cannot and will not change. Man changes constantly to fit in and feel accepted by the general population. The '70s had a saying, "I am in with the in crowd" and that made us feel cool. So, if the crowd decides to go to hell, then by all means let's go, if we can look cool in the process.

This is the real deal. Society is trying to make us believe that homosexual relationships are normal and okay in the eyes of man and God. As I stated earlier, man will always change his beliefs to suit his needs at the time, but God will never change his rules for living. If we confess that we are a Christian and we believe that the Holy Bible is the true word of God, in which he directly states his displeasure with the gay lifestyle, then why do we feel God created it and it is normal and free from judgment?

Why are we becoming so accepting of homosexuality when it is something that God, who we say we love and serve, passionately rejects? The following is my theory, which I put together from a story I heard told by the late Rev. Billy Graham many years ago. I will call it *"the theory of the boiling frog."*

If we place a frog into a pot of boiling water, it will react to it quickly by jumping out to save itself from the deadly situation. Now, put that same frog in a pot of cool water, were the conditions seem normal and comfortable, then turn the heat up very slowly. The water will gradually warm up with each slight turn of the control until the water starts to boil and the frog eventually dies. Please do not try to test this theory at home, but simply have faith in the science behind it.

So, what is causing us to be more accepting of this ungodly lifestyle? The devil has his demonic hand on the temperature control of morality, and we do not even know it. The outcome will be the same: we will slowly begin to die spiritually and eventually our souls will be lost. Christians who operate in homosexuality must realize that God is telling us that it is time to jump out of this sexually perverted pot before it is too late. Do we really think this problem is just going to disappear? When we have a serious problem with our car and we fail to get it fixed, does the problem just vanish? Then, why should we treat this social problem any differently? We must face the fact that this lifestyle is wrong in the sight of God and then find the courage as well as the strength to fix it in a godly manner.

A lot of the problems that we experience in today's society, whether they be physical or spiritual in nature, can be linked to some kind of sexual issue or event in our lives. It does not matter if it's homosexuality, bisexuality, infidelity, incest, rape, sodomy, abortion, adultery, or the lack of sexual contact with a loved one by way of rejection or death. It will require a tremendous amount of prayer for healing these types of wounds.

Think about this for a moment. A young couple have three wonderful God-loving children. Every Sunday, the family goes to church to honor God for all the blessings in their lives and prays before each meal that they share together. One day, while out on a dinner date without the kids, the two suffered a fatal car accident. They did not put anything in their will to state who would care for the kids in the event something like this would happen. No close relatives can be located, so the kids have to go into foster care until they can be legally adopted. How would you feel if this was your situation and the adopting couple was gay? What kind of environment would your children be raised in? If you think that this is impossible, well, I hate to tell you, but it is already happening. Now, your child's view on what is normal will change. Satan's hand is on the dial.

God has already stated his rules and laws when it comes to sex, but for some reason, we try to bend them in order to satisfy our own fleshly desires. So, when we give in to our flesh, we open the door for Satan's curses, which make our lives a living *hell*.

God states that all sex is a sin, and it is *only* accepted between a married man and a woman. Therefore, if we are sexually active outside of the institution of marriage, then we are living in sin. Now, if we are in a homosexual relationship, then God views that as an abomination to what he created men and women for. It would be like slapping God in the face. What do you think his reaction would be to that?

> *For the wages of sin is death, but the gift of God is eternal life in[a] Christ Jesus our Lord. (Romans 6:23)*

Homosexuality is an abominable sin outside of a God-ordained marriage that he will never accept, and it will come with a very high price. So, other than possible monetary benefits from the world's system and a false sense of security, it is a deadly situation to place one's self in spiritually. Is this type of intimate relationship really worth the loss of our soul? We define a wage as a fitting return or payment in exchange for something given or done. Godly obedience will save our soul and offer the gift of eternal life.

In the June 28, 2006, edition of USA Today, section D, page one, there was an article written by Gary Levin titled *Underserved* where viewers get a new gay channel. He stated that Logo, MTV Networks' long planned basic-cable channel, is planning to launch it on June 30, along with Here! TV and Q Television, a digital cable network that will be available to around forty-four million homes around the country. This project is backed by a media conglomerate, which includes the major cable network Viacom.

One of the programs that aired as a series was titled *Noah's Arc*. This program follows the lives of four gay men living in Los Angeles. This drama was a "Sex in the City" style show but with four gay male characters. Although this program ran for only one season, the families who purchase cable and Direct TV had access to this channel. The average homeowner never knew they had it until they or their children discovered it accidentally while channel surfing. This may prove to be a great shock to the unsuspecting viewer or their unmonitored child because some of the scenes were really sexually graphic.

> *Start children off on the way they should go, and*
> *even when they are old they will not turn from it.*
> *(Proverbs 22:6)*

We as a Christian society should continue to pursue the will of God by keeping the law that he has given us. The direction in which our country is headed, as it relates to homosexuality, is one of certain failure in the long run because that's what God has stated as the consequence of disobedience in this matter. Parents, with all the TVs in our homes and with all the channels to surf, how can we guarantee that our child is not viewing this type of programming right now?

The words in the song "The Greatest Love of All," written by Linda Creed and Michael Masser, states, "I believe the children are our future. Teach them well and help them lead the way. Show them all the beauty they possess inside." This to me is simply prophetic in terms of godly directions. If we raise our child the way God wants us to, the gay lifestyle would be far less appealing to them when they are grown. Then, they would be the spiritual advocates against this growing social issue.

According to the Williams Project at UCLA, which ended on June 19, 2016, the gay, lesbian, bisexual, and transgender population in the United States is up by 7% in adults, but the percentage is higher in certain large metropolitan cities, such as, San Francisco, New York City, Atlanta, Key West, and Los Angeles, to name a few.

Parliament passed The Marriage (Same Sex Couples) Act 2013 that would give gays the right to get married by changing the definition of a couple from a man and a woman to just two people. The Netherlands (2000), Belgium (2003), Canada (2005), Spain (2005), South Africa (2006), Norway and Sweden (2009), Argentina, Iceland and Portugal (2010), Denmark (2012), Brazil, England, Wales, France, New Zealand and Uruguay (2013), Luxembourg (2014), Finland (signed 2015, effective 2017), and Ireland (2015).

In America, the law is recognized from state to state. These states are Alabama, Alaska, Arizona, California, Colorado, Connecticut, Delaware, Florida, Hawaii, Idaho, Illinois, Indiana, Iowa, Kansas, Maine, Maryland, Massachusetts, Minnesota, Montana, Nevada, New Hampshire, New Jersey, New Mexico, New York, North Carolina, Oklahoma, Oregon, Pennsylvania, Rhode Island, South Carolina, Utah, Vermont, Virginia, Washington, West Virginia, Wisconsin, and Wyoming. Most other states had enacted constitutional or statutory bans on same-sex marriage known as "Defense of Marriage" Acts.

This issue of homosexuality is the center of a lot of pain and suffering for many individuals and their families and friends. It has destroyed some of these relationships completely, while others are hanging by an emotional thread.

The gay lifestyle is all about self-gratification by ungodly means and self-righteousness, which has never been pleasing to God. Most are not born with this mindset but develop it over time from worldly experiences and physical perceptions. For any Christian to say that they were born gay is to say God made a mistake during their birth, and that would be one of the most hypocritical statements a child of God could make. God never makes mistakes.

A simple way to prove this is the fact that God created man and woman for the purpose of reproduction of his kind, so they could be of service to him. Since there is no possibility of reproduction in a homosexual relationship, then what would be God's purpose in creating this mindset? Everything God designs has a divine purpose and is done for a specific reason. Each person he creates has a destiny with a purpose that is designed to serve his holy kingdom. Do not let the world trick you into believing that you are something other than what God was created you to be. If we become confused about what we are and what we are here for, then we should realize the root of our confusion.

> *For God is not a God of disorder but of peace—*
> *as in all the congregation of the Lord's people.*
> *(1 Corinthians 14:33)*

This Scripture lets us know that those who are living in confusion with regard to their sexuality and find it hard to find inner peace are experiencing something that is not from God rather from Satan, who is the author confusion and the father of lies.

When I was growing up, gay boys were teased and taunted severely by the kids at school and in the neighborhood. The gay girls were simply left alone, literally. I did not agree with the ill treatment of this group of lost souls, but the spirit of man at that time casted a judgement on them that's similar to God's, which was condemnation and separation. However, through repentance, God will forgive and show mercy, while the mindset of man is to operate in condemnation.

Today, with the growth of the gay movement, it appears that society's attitude is changing rapidly toward general acceptance of this culture. Before, men and women were afraid to be known as homosexuals because of the judgment that was placed on them by men, but they had no fear of the judgment from God. Now, they have very little fear of the judgment from God or man, and they are starting to feel more comfortable in this lifestyle. This broadened comfort zone has spilled onto the mindset of the younger generation who feels that the gay lifestyle is no big deal.

The outcome of this spiritually diluted view of sexual morality is that sexually active teenagers are using it as a way of hiding their activities by having sex within small groups of the same gender. This way, the parents will not question the amount of time they are spending together with their circle of friends. This action is mostly found within female groups more often than males. The problem arises when the desire to be with someone of the same sex starts to grow in his or her spirit. Once this type of subconscious thought process starts growing, it will never stop until God uproots it by way of faith and personal repentance.

What I foresee happening with this generation is that they will start experimenting with this ungodly sexual activity for personal sexual relief due to their early start. Some will walk away and move on to normal sexual behavior, while others will develop emotional ties to their past partners as well as the lifestyle itself. This will cause great confusion in their spiritual lives, which will ultimately lead to physical depression and despair.

The individuals who walk away from this lifestyle and eventually meet the person of their dreams but do not seek God for repentance and deliverance from this ungodly spirit will pay a price in future relationships. The new love in their life finds out about their gay past, feeling hurt and deceived, ends the relationship. Now, they are brokenhearted and emotionally bruised. Then, one day, they receive a call of comfort from one of their gay partners from the past, which sends them right back into this abominably, sinful way of life.

What people fail to realize is that we have got to start living righteously, pure, and holy before God. This is done by knowing his word, doing his will, and walking in his way. This way, when something ungodly is presented to us, our spirit can discern whether it is right or wrong in the eyes of God the father. This gives us the power and authority to resist this form of temptation.

> *No temptation has overtaken you except what is common to mankind. And God is faithful; he will not let you be tempted[b] beyond what you can bear. But when you are tempted, [c] he will also provide a way out so that you can endure it. (1 Corinthians 10:13)*

Let's seek the righteousness of God for the spiritual cure to this issue by dealing with it as a social problem that the devil created and only God can solve. We can no longer let the world define our moral values for us, but rather let us live holy lives ourselves and set ourselves as godly examples for others to fellow. This sinful, worldly physical attraction does not have to be spiritually fatal, because through Jesus Christ, we can be healed. He is the living first aid for this sinful condition called homosexuality. We cannot start to heal until we accept the diagnosis and sign off on God's treatment plan. He is waiting for us to make the appointment to be whole again.

Story: Joe's Dilemma

Joe is a member of his high-school soccer team together with his good friend Bobby. It is time for the prom, so Joe asks a young lady named Connie if she would like to go with him, and she says "yes," because she has always liked Joe since middle school.

Connie spends the next few weeks making preparations for the big event by buying the gown, picking out shoes, getting her hair fixed, and, finally, with her mom's assistance, putting on the makeup. She does not want to disappoint Joe, her dream date.

Now, Joe too is getting ready. He picked up his tuxedo, got his hair cut, and washed the car inside and out. Joe is ready to go and pick up his beautiful prom date. He arrives on time, they take lots of pictures, go out to eat, and finally make it to the big dance.

As they sit at their table, enjoying the moment, Connie still can't believe that she is here at her senior prom with Joe. They dance and talk throughout the evening, but Joe's mind has always been somewhere else. Just across the room is the true love of his life. It is someone who he has had feelings for a long time. Why did he not ask this person to be his date at such a memorable event? He could not because the person that he loves is his best friend Bobby.

This story is being played out every day, in many different ways, all over the world. As a Christian, we believe that the word of God is total truth and Jesus Christ is this word in the flesh. If Joe is a born-again believer, then he has the ability to ask God for anything: "Ask and it will be given to you" (Matthew 7:7). The word also says, "I can do all this through him who gives me strength." (Philippians 4:13). So, why can't God help Joe to be with Bobby? It is because the request is outside the will of God and out of line with his word.

To ask anything from God, it has to line up with the word that he has given us, because *he only gives good and perfect gifts* (James 1:17). Since this relationship is outside the will of God, he cannot bless it, but he will not stop us from pursuing this lifestyle on our own. He just wants us to know that if we do, we are totally on our own. The holy hedge of protection is gone. It's like sailing out to sea without a life vest, map or compass in the boat. Live at your own risk.

If we own a car, we know that most states require us to have auto insurance before we can operate the vehicle. If we are stopped by the police or have an accident without it, there will be a heavy price to pay. Insurance is for our protection as well as for the people around us. Its purpose is to help place us back in the same position, with transportation, finances, and health, which we were in before the accident occurred.

Grace and mercy are God's insurance policy benefits to us. The premium is our obedience to his laws and commandments. Just like letting our car insurance policy lapse, the consequences will be the same, and that is having no protection for life's negative events. Choose your spiritual coverage wisely. Do not let lifestyle choices cause your policy to lapse with God. Accidents will always happen, but God is the only one who can make us whole again. The premium may seem high, but the coverage is truly a divine blessing.

A Prayer for Righteousness

Gracious and merciful God, we know that we have wandered from you and have sinned against your name. To our shame, we have obeyed our sinful lust and have broken your laws and commandments. We have missed the mark of righteousness and holy living; we have done that which you have commanded us not to perform. We ask for your deliverance, forgiveness and your mercy. Restore unto us the joy of your salvation and accept our repentance according to your loving kindness. Give us now the assurance that our sins have been forgiven and you will remember them no more. In the loving name of Jesus Christ, we pray. Amen.

Key Scriptures

Please read the entire chapter of each verse for greater edification and understanding.

1. *Genesis: 19:1–13*
2. *Leviticus 18:22*
3. *Hebrews 13:8*
4. *Romans 4:18*
5. *Hebrews 11:17–18*
6. *Romans 6:23*
7. *Proverbs 22:6*
8. *1 Corinthians 14:33*
9. *1 Corinthians 10:13*
10. *James1:17*

CHAPTER ELEVEN

The Blind Soldier

Join with me in suffering, like a good soldier of Christ Jesus. 4 No one serving as a soldier gets entangled in civilian affairs, but rather tries to please his commanding officer. (2 Timothy 2:3–4)

A soldier cannot win the fight if they continually go into battle without the right training, armor, weapons, and leadership. An unequipped warrior who does not follow the orders of their commanding officer, will always be left fighting alone, unprepared and unequipped. This unfortunate combatant being described here is you and I, when we become blinded by the affairs and circumstances of this world and not walking by faith in God's word for our protection, healing and victory in this battle called life.

A pastor once stated that Christians are the only soldiers who come to the battle already wounded, bleeding, and broken. The meaning behind this descriptive analysis is that we can't be effective soldiers for God if, when life inflicts us with pain and suffering, our lack of faith causes us to accept defeat mentally, physically and spiritually well before the real battle begins.

The main survival tools of a soldier is knowledge of the enemy and the ability to use the weapons at their disposal. The more confident they feel in these two areas of warfare, the greater their chances are of survival and success on the field in battle.

It is a known fact that confidence comes from faith and our ability to visualize victory at the start of any given situation. This faith will guide us through the times when the tide seems to be changing against us, but we must continue to hold fast until the end. Also, this level of faith will help us overcome the doubt of others around us, who have already started waving the symbolic white flag declaring defeat.

> *Now faith is confidence in what we hope for and assurance about what we do not see. (Hebrews 11:1)*

Every day that God blesses us with the strength to wake up with a clear mind and healthy body is another opportunity to be of service to him. Whenever we decide to serve God, we automatically become an enemy of Satan. Just like in any war, the enemy's main objective is to claim victory over us. This is why we need to know as much about him as he knows about us. Satan has knowledge of all of our needs and desires, just like God. The devil uses this information to keep us distracted with worldly vices, which ultimately distracts us from the destiny that God has designed for our lives.

These are God's holy laws which were defined in chapter two, that he gave us to live by. If we are obedient in these ten areas during our daily battles, then he will protect us, so the devil will not have the victory.

The Ten Commandments

1. *Love God first, with all our being.*
2. *Love all others as ourselves.*
3. *Honor the Sabbath day.*
4. *Honor our mother and father.*
5. *Do not kill.*
6. *Do not steal.*
7. *Do not lie.*
8. *Do not worship other idols.*

9. *Do not commit adultery.*
10. *Do not covet anything or anyone.*
    (Exodus 20:1–17; Matthews: 19:18–19)

These are the weapons in Satan's arsenal, which is based on one main character defect, physical addictions:

1. *Money*
2. *Drugs*
3. *Alcohol*
4. *Cigarettes*
5. *Sex*
6. *Food*
7. *Clothes*
8. *Vehicles*
9. *Gambling*
10. *Work*
11. *TV*
12. *Sports*

If being obedient to God will keep us strong in battle, then what would cause us to drop our guard in the midst of a fight for life or death. The most commonly broken commandments are 1, 2, 3, 5, 6, 7, 8, 9, and 10

- Cheating on tax returns (6–7)
- Taking money and materials from our job (6)
- Borrowing money and things with no intention of returning it (7–10)
- Using the ideas of others to advance our position (10)
- Continuously living off our parents and others after we've become adults (10)
- Fraudulently using the government welfare system for personal gain. (6–7)
- Spending more time and money on entertainment than God (9)

- Filing false claims and law suits for profit (6–7)
- Sex outside marriage (8)
- Selling or buying bootleg or copyright protected merchandise (6 & 10)
- Road rage (2)
- Taking someone's life (5)
- Working on Sunday by choice and never worshiping God in his house (1,3)

All of these things are considered by most of us to be a part of everyday life. We do it so often that it no longer seems wrong. These problems are the result of us forgetting God's laws and like "The theory of the boiling frog" in chapter 10, we become comfortable with our sin. Do you see yourself in any of these categories?

Every one of the items listed above represents a type of flesh weakness that we try to satisfy by worldly means. Whether it is trying to feel, look, or live better, it really does not matter when we are looking for solutions in ungodly ways. The outcome of this type of ungodly behavior will ultimately lead to spiritual death, thus leaving us no real reason to continue our physical existence on this earth. Because, once the spirit dies, we can no longer be of service to God. If we are not serving God, then we must be serving Satan.

Some of the warning signs that we are losing the battle of life and heading down the road of self-destruction will be in the form of abusing others, trouble in our marriage, uncontrollable children, termination from a job due to rule violations, loss of property, serious self-imposed financial problems, sickness, and death. All of these can be the result of our disobedient spirit, which leads us to ungodly behavior.

> *And the peace of God, which transcends all understanding, will guard your hearts and your minds in Christ Jesus. (Philippians 4:7)*

If we are seeking peace, joy, and happiness through some form of worldly addiction, then we have failed before we even get started.

Anything that we acquire from the world to feel good will always be temporary. It is just a false promise of relief to our emotional pain. All godly remedies are eternal and everlasting.

God is the father of truth, and the devil is the father of lies. Anything that is false in nature is not godly and therefore a product of the devil's worldly system.

> *He is the Rock, his works are perfect, and all his ways are just: A faithful God who does no wrong, upright and just is he. (Deuteronomy 32:4)*
>
> *You belong to your father, the devil, and you want to carry out your father's desires. He was a murderer from the beginning, not holding to the truth, for there is no truth in him. When he lies, he speaks his native language, for he is a liar and the father of lies. (John 8:44)*

Here, we have two totally different fathers. One influences our spirit for the purpose of good, while the other controls the flesh for the purpose of evil. As it is physically impossible to have two earthly fathers, neither can we serve two spiritually.

> *No one can serve two masters. Either you will hate the one and love the other, or you will be devoted to the one and despise the other. You cannot serve both God and money. (Mathew 6:24)*

Until we decide which master we wish to serve, we will never achieve real victory in our lives. As the word of God has stated many times, there is no gray area concerning his will for our lives. We are either for him or against him, and the choice is always ours to make.

I remember when I was young and attending our small family church, every now and then, we would have a testimonial service that allowed anyone to stand and testify about a special blessing that they had received from God. I never stood to speak back then because I did not feel my life experiences were important enough to mention. Now,

I have grown to learn that before each real testimony there was a real test from God, and our faith is the only thing that will allow us to pass that type of test. When we are tested, we have to be ready to do battle without being blind to our enemies' tactics. We need the whole armor of God to survive this war. (please review God's armor in chapter one)

We need to start praying daily for God to give us wisdom, knowledge, and understanding that will enable us to see more clearly the battles before us as well as recognize the enemies that live within our own camp. The battles of life, at times, can be so great that we just feel like giving up and waving the white flag. However, we must keep a strong, healthy spirit and continue to develop our faith in God and his son Jesus Christ. When we do this, we will always be able to claim the victory in every battle that we face.

> *He gives strength to the weary and increases the power of the weak.*
>
> *Even youths grow tired and weary, and young men stumble and fall;*
>
> **but those who hope in the Lord will renew their strength. They will soar on wings like eagles; they will run and not grow weary, they will walk and not be faint.** *(Isaiah 40:29–31)*

We are all soldiers in God's holy army. He will give us all the necessary tools and weapons we need to compete on life's battle field. Our sole mission is to serve him by serving others with our time, talents and resources. If God is your commander and chief then, just follow his orders and we will know that no battle is too great for us to win, or opponent too strong for us to defeat. We are God's soldiers, his word is the first aid on the battlefield and Jesus is the key to our Victory.

The Lord's Prayer

Our Father in heaven, hallowed be your name, your kingdom come, your will be done, on earth as it is in heaven. Give us today our daily bread. And forgive us our debts, as we also have forgiven our debtors. And lead us not into temptation, but deliver us from the evil one. For Thine is the kingdom, and the power, and the glory forever and ever. Amen (*Mathew 6:9–13*).

Key Scriptures

Please read the entire chapter of each verse for greater edification and understanding.

1. *2 Timothy 2:3–4*
2. *Hebrews 11:1*
3. *Exodus 20:1–17*
4. *Matthews: 19:18–19*
5. *Philippians 4:7*
6. *Deuteronomy 32:4*
7. *John 8:44*
8. *Isaiah 40:29–31*
9. *Mathew 6:9–13*

THE FIRST BOOK OF JAMES

New International Version (NIV)

The book of James, written by the half-brother of Jesus Christ, is a holy guide to righteous living. I would strongly encourage you to read all five chapters to receive its wealth of knowledge and godly wisdom that will help you in your daily living. I will start you off with a breakdown of chapter one, and hopefully, it will feed your spirit to study the remaining four.

1 *James, a servant of God and of the Lord Jesus Christ,*
To the twelve tribes scattered among the nations: Greetings. James 1:1

He starts the letter off by stating first and foremost that he was a servant; meaning, his sole purpose is to be obedient to God and his son Jesus and do what they created him for. Remember what Jesus said to God in the garden of Gethsemane, not my will but thy will be done.

Trials and Temptations

2 *Consider it pure joy, my brothers and sisters,[a] whenever you face trials of many kinds, 3 because you know that the testing of your faith produces perseverance. 4 Let perseverance finish its work so that you may be mature and complete, not lacking anything. James 1:2-4*

Verses two through four: They speak of the fact that life's problems and worldly temptations are not given to you by God but are used by him to test and strengthen your faith and develop self-confidence. There can never be a testimony without a real test. The more difficult the test, the greater degree of satisfaction you will receive when it is finished. The sharpest swords cannot be created without hours of grinding and polishing. The resistance is part of the perfecting process. God will never present you with more resistance than you can bear, because He knows your limits.

5 If any of you lacks wisdom, you should ask God, who gives generously to all without finding fault, and it will be given to you. 6 But when you ask, you must believe and not doubt, because the one who doubts is like a wave of the sea, blown and tossed by the wind. 7 That person should not expect to receive anything from the Lord. 8 Such a person is double-minded and unstable in all they do. James 1:5-8

Verses five through eight: We all will encounter things that we just don't understand all the time. Whether it is on the job, at school, in a relationship, or at church, confusion is going to arise. God tells us to ask him for all the answers to our problems, but we must be willing to trust his advice. If you do not trust him, then you must trust someone else, but you must choose which way you are going. Fence straddling usually ends in pain.

9 Believers in humble circumstances ought to take pride in their high position. 10 But the rich should take pride in their humiliation—since they will pass away like a wild flower. 11 For the sun rises with scorching heat and withers the plant; its blossom falls and its beauty is destroyed. In the same way, the rich will fade away even while they go about their business. James 1:9-11

Verses nine through eleven: Here, he is saying that you should feel grateful when you are poor and blessed if you are well off. Poverty will humble you because of your lack of resources, but do not let this state of being weaken your faith in God, as he is still walking with you every day. If you have wealth, then you must thank him daily for this blessing and never get to the place that you feel that you got to this state of increase alone. Without a humble spirit, just like the flower, it can be gone.

12 Blessed is the one who perseveres under trial because, having stood the test, that person will receive the crown of life that the Lord has promised to those who love him. James 1:12

Verse twelve: God said that he has a special blessing for you every time you face troubles and handle them in a godly way. He rewards you for good behavior.

13 When tempted, no one should say, "God is tempting me." For God cannot be tempted by evil, nor does he tempt anyone; 14 but each person is tempted when they are dragged away by their own evil desire and enticed. 15 Then, after desire has conceived, it gives birth to sin; and sin, when it is full-grown, gives birth to death. James 1:13-15

Verses thirteen through fifteen: If you are ever tempted to do anything ungodly, then you can rest assured the thing that is tempting you did not come from God. He cannot use evil things to test you and the degree of your faith, but he will reward your resistance to it. Failing to resist evil temptations will give way to a sinful action, and a sinful action brings on God's judgment. Without true repentance for the sin, your spirit will become weak and the body cannot exist without it.

16 Don't be deceived, my dear brothers and sisters. 17 Every good and perfect gift is from above, coming down from the Father of the heavenly lights, who does not change like shifting shadows. 18 He chose to give us birth through the word of truth, that we might be a kind of first fruits of all he created. James 1:16-18

Verses sixteen through eighteen: When you receive anything that is good for your mind, body, or soul, then it came from God. If it only brings you suffering, misery, and pain, then it is definitely due to one of Satan's worldly vices. The fact that God does not change will not allow him to offer you anything but that which is only meant for your good. When we accept his word and his son Jesus Christ, we are born again and become a first fruit offering unto him. We become his holy child.

Listening and Doing

19 My dear brothers and sisters, take note of this: Everyone should be quick to listen, slow to speak and slow to become angry, 20 because human anger does not produce the righteousness that God desires. 21 Therefore, get rid of all moral filth and the evil that is so prevalent and humbly accept the word planted in you, which can save you. James 1:19-21

Verses nineteen through twenty-one: Here, he addresses a major problem in today's society and that is the failure to communicate with one another. We should listen more carefully, speak with more compassion, and then take a little time to think before we act. We can only do this if we have the word of God in our hearts and minds. This course of action will surly cut down on the sins from over reacting.

22 Do not merely listen to the word, and so deceive yourselves. Do what it says. 23 Anyone who listens to the word but does not do what it says is like someone who looks at his face in a mirror 24 and, after looking at himself, goes away and immediately forgets what he looks like. 25 But whoever looks intently into the perfect law that gives freedom, and continues in it—not forgetting what they have heard, but doing it—they will be blessed in what they do. James 1:22-25

Verses twenty-two through twenty-five: God does not want us to only reverence him but also respect his word by living it through our daily actions toward one another. Like the man who forgot the image he saw in the mirror, we must learn to study his word more closely so that we can draw from its wisdom when the time arises. This will be a blessing to you and others around you.

26 Those who consider themselves religious and yet do not keep a tight rein on their tongues deceive themselves, and their religion is worthless. 27 Religion that God our Father accepts as pure and faultless is this: to look after orphans and widows in their distress and to keep oneself from being polluted by the world. James 1:26-27

Verses twenty-six through twenty-seven: In conclusion, if you consider yourself a born-again Christian, then your actions should demonstrate the faith that you confess to have in a positive way. Others around you should be able to tell that you are different. Your spirit should be a form of light in any place or situation when you are present. God wants us to help anyone who is unable to help themselves, regardless of their race, creed, sex, or religious beliefs. Just remember, WWJD, what would Jesus do?

IMAGINE!

By David A. Rose, Sr.

Imagine this if you can
When we pass away
Our body slowly lowered into the ground
Or our ashes placed on public display.

But our spirit
Will live Forever
Where?
Our faith, works and living will decide.

Imagine it in Heaven,
With streets of gold and pearly gates.
Hearing heavenly sounds of joyous praise
And only peaceful days await.

Now, Imagine it in Hell,
In the mist of darkness
With lakes of fire
Where only pain and suffering abides.

If death were to appear
At this very moment in time
We know where our body will be.
But what about our spirit,
What destiny have we prepared for it to see?

We've, Imagined it in Hell
With an all-consuming fire and never-ending pain
We've, Imagined it in Heaven
With everlasting joy and peace
All the time singing praises to his holy name.

So, live a life that pleases God
And our spirit will be free
To be with him forever.
In peace and eternal harmony

Imagine!
Eternal life,
Everlasting peace,
And unspeakable joy
Just Imagine That!

Opening the Door to Salvation

If you do not have a personal relationship with God and never accepted his son Jesus Christ as your Lord and savior, who was born of a virgin and suffered death on the cross because of his beliefs and teachings. He was placed in a tomb where he stayed for three days, then he rose from the dead with a new body. He then ascended in into heaven to join his father until a day of judgment. If you can believe this with all our mind, body, and spirit and confess it with your mouth, then You Are Saved! Now, read the following prayer of salvation out loud so that you can confess your belief to God.

Prayer of Salvation

If you do not know Jesus as your Savior and Lord, simply pray the following prayer in faith, and Jesus will be your Lord!

*Heavenly Father, I come to You in the Name of Jesus. Your Word says, "Whosoever shall call on the name of the Lord shall be saved" (**Acts 2:21**). I am calling on You. I pray and ask Jesus to come into my heart and be Lord over my life according to **Romans 10:9-10**: "If thou shalt confess with thy mouth the Lord Jesus, and shalt believe in thine heart that God has raised him from the dead, thou shalt be saved. For with the heart man believeth unto righteousness; and with the mouth confession is made unto salvation." I do that now. I confess that Jesus is Lord, and I believe in my heart that God raised Him from the dead.*

*I am now reborn! I am a Christian—a child of Almighty God! I am saved! You also said in Your Word, "If ye then being evil, know how to give good gifts unto your children: HOW MUCH MORE shall your heavenly Father give the Holy Spirit to them that ask him?" (**Luke 11:13**). I'm also asking You to fill me with the Holy Spirit. Holy Spirit, rise up within me as I praise God. I fully expect to speak with other tongues as You give me the utterance (**Acts 2:4**). In Jesus' Name. Amen.*

This prayer of salvation was taken from the website of www.kcm.org for Kenneth Copeland Ministries

If you decide to give your life to Jesus Christ, please e-mail me at Firstaid4thespirit@gmail.com so I can pray for you and your rebirth in Christ. Also send me the name of your new church home. Be Blessed Always.

THE BLESSING OF GIVING

In everything I did, I showed you that by this kind of hard work we must help the weak, remembering the words the Lord Jesus himself said: "It is more blessed to give than to receive" (Act 20:35)

It is my sincere hope that this writing has been a blessing to you and that it has enabled you to find areas of your life that are in need of spiritual healing and that it will unblock every blessing which God has waiting for you.

First Aid for the Spirit was written as a simple guide for you to follow to know what God requires of us to be blessed and to point out the things that are not pleasing to him, while drawing attention to areas that will cause us to lose sight of his word and his will for us and our destiny. So, if you feel that this book has been a blessing to you, then I encourage you to use God's spirit of giving and bless others with a copy. This may be a soul you save, and a spirit you help to heal. Remember, God always rewards a cheerful giver.

Stay spiritually healthy and blessed.

Truly yours,
David A. Rose, Sr.

GLOSSARY OF THE GOSPEL

In all thou ways get understanding.

1. Abomination: something regarded with disgust or hatred: something <u>abominable</u> <*considered war an abomination,* extreme disgust and hatred of
2. Adultery: voluntary sexual intercourse between a married man and someone other than his wife or between a married woman and someone other than her husband
3. Angel: (1) one of a class of spiritual beings; a celestial attendant of God. (2) a messenger, especially of God. (3) an attendant or guardian spirit.
4. Anointed: to choose by or as if by divine election
5. Baptize: to purify or cleanse spiritually especially by a purging experience or ordeal
6. Blessing: help and approval from God, something that helps you or brings happiness
7. Born Again: having a new or stronger belief in the Christian religion
8. Condemnation: a statement or expression of very strong and definite criticism or disapproval
9. Covet: (1) To wish or desire for enviously. (2) To wish, long or hope for, with the painful or resentful awareness of an advantage enjoyed by another, along with the desire to possess the same advantage.
10. Creator: a person who makes something new
11. Curse: a prayer or invocation for harm or injury to come upon one, a profane or obscene oath or word, evil or mis-

fortune that comes as if in response to <u>imprecation</u> or as retribution

12. Demon: an evil spirit, a source or agent of evil, harm, distress, or ruin

13. Deliverance: deliverance from the power and effects of sin *b*: the agent or means that effects salvation

14. Devil: the personal supreme spirit of evil often represented in Jewish and Christian belief as the tempter of humankind, the leader of all apostate angels, and the ruler of hell, the most powerful spirit of evil in Christianity,

15. Drunkenness: pertaining to, caused by, or marked by intoxication

16. Emulation: ambitious or envious rivalry

17. Envying: painful or resentful awareness of an advantage enjoyed by another joined with a desire to possess the same advantage

18. Faith: belief and trust in and loyalty to God *(2)*: belief in the traditional <u>doctrines</u> of a religion *b (1)* : firm belief in something for which there is no proof *(2)* : complete trust

19. Favor: friendly regard shown toward another especially by a superior *(2)*: approving consideration or attention, gracious kindness, a special privilege or right granted or conceded

20. Fear: to have a reverential awe

21. First fruit; the earliest gathered fruits offered to the Deity in acknowledgment of the gift of fruitfulness. To give the best that you have.

22. Fornication: consensual sexual intercourse between two persons not married to each other

23. Giving: to put into the possession of another for his or her use, to administer as a sacrament, to commit to another as a trust or responsibility and usually for an expressed reason

24. God: the Being perfect in power, wisdom, and goodness who is worshipped as creator and ruler of the universe, a being or object believed to have more than natural attributes and powers and to require human worship; *specifically*: one controlling a particular aspect or part of reality

25. Grace: unmerited divine assistance given humans for their regeneration or sanctification *b*: a virtue coming from God *c*: a state of sanctification enjoyed through divine assistance
26. Hate: intense hostility and <u>aversion</u> usually deriving from fear, anger, or sense of injury *b*: extreme dislike or disgust
27. Heresy: an opinion, doctrine, or practice contrary to the truth or to generally accepted beliefs or standards
28. Holy Spirit: the third person of the Christian Trinity, God in the form of a spirit in Christianity, the Father, the Son, and the *Holy Spirit,* called also *the Holy Ghost or comforter.*
29. Honor: good name or public <u>esteem</u>, a showing of usually <u>merited</u> respect, an evidence or symbol of distinction
30. Hope: to cherish a desire with anticipation: to want something to happen or be true, to expect with confidence
    a. Idolatry: the worship of a physical object as a god
    b. immoderate attachment or devotion to something
31. Jesus Christ: the Jewish religious teacher whose life, death, and resurrection as reported by the Evangelists are the basis of the Christian message of salvation
32. Joy: the emotion evoked by well-being, success, or good fortune or by the prospect of possessing what one desires:
    a. Lascivious: filled with or showing sexual desire
    b. Love: unselfish loyal and benevolent concern for the good of another: such as *(1)*: the fatherly concern of God for humankind *(2)*: brotherly concern for others *b*: a person's adoration of God
33. Lust: usually intense or unbridled sexual desire, an intense longing
34. Mercy: a blessing that is an act of divine favor or compassion
35. Murder: the crime of unlawfully killing a person especially with malice <u>aforethought</u>, something very difficult or dangerous, something outrageous or blameworthy
36. Obedience: an act or instance of obeying *b*: the quality or state of being <u>obedient</u>

37. Offering: something <u>offered</u>; *especially*: a sacrifice ceremonially offered as a part of worship *c* : a contribution to the support of a church
38. Pride: inordinate self-esteem: <u>conceit</u> *b*: a reasonable or justifiable self-respect *c*: delight or elation arising from some act, possession, or relationship
39. Repentance: the action or process of <u>repenting</u> especially for misdeeds or moral shortcomings
40. Resurrection: the rising of Christ from the dead
41. Reveling; to take intense pleasure or satisfaction
42. Sacrifice: an act of offering to a deity something precious; destruction or surrender of something for the sake of something else
43. Salvation: deliverance from the power and effects of sin *b*: the agent or means that effects salvation
44. Satan: The grand adversary of man the devil or prince of darkness the chief of the fallen angels
45. Sin: The voluntary departure of a moral agent from a known rule of rectitude or duty, prescribed by God any voluntary transgression of the divine law, or violation of divine command a wicked act iniquity. It is either a positive act in which a known divine law is violated, or it is the voluntary neglect to obey a positive divine command, or a rule or a rule of duty clearly implied in such command.
46. Steal: to take the property of another wrongfully and especially as a habitual or regular practice, to appropriate to oneself or beyond one's proper share: make oneself the focus of *<steal the show>*
    a. Strife: bitter sometimes violent conflict or dissension *<political strife>b* : an act of contention : <u>fight</u>, <u>struggle</u> exertion or contention for superiority
47. Surrender: to yield to the power, control, or possession of another upon compulsion or demand, to give (oneself) over to something (as an influence)
    a. Temptation; the act of <u>tempting</u> or the state of being <u>tempted</u> especially to evil : <u>enticement</u>

  b.   something tempting: a cause or occasion of enticement
48. Testimony: an open acknowledgment **b**: a public profession of religious experience
  a.   Tithes: to pay or give a tenth part of especially for the support of a religious establishment or organization to levy a tithe on
49. Trinity; the unity of Father, Son, and Holy Spirit as three persons in one Godhead according to Christian dogma
50. Trust: a charge or duty imposed in faith or confidence or as a condition of some relationship *(2)*: something committed or entrusted to one to be used or cared for in the interest of another
  a.   Unclean; morally or spiritually impure
  b.   infected with a harmful supernatural contagion; *also*: prohibited by ritual law for use or contact
51. Variance: the fact or state of being in disagreement, not in harmony or agreement
52. Wrath: retributory punishment for an offense or a crime: divine chastisement
53. Witchcraft: the use of sorcery or magic **b:** communication with the devil or with a familiar **c:** an irresistible influence or fascination with dark powers

About the Author

I was born in Roanoke, Virginia, to two loving, caring, Christian parents. They gave my sister, brother, and I a solid foundation on how to become godly human beings. This was achieved by strict discipline and direction based mainly on their faith and how they had been raised. We mainly attended my mother's small family church, Bethel A.M. E., Cave Spring, which was in Roanoke county and cofounded by my great, great grandfather Boyer Beane.

Once a month, we would go to my father's church, High Street Baptist, which was in the city and on occasion, we would walk from our home. Both were good churches to hear the word of God, but I was just too young to fully understand what I was hearing. Even when I became older, my depth of knowledge of the gospel was extremely limited. I just didn't know how to apply what I was hearing to real life situations.

Five months into my job with the airlines in 1981, I met my soul mate, Vicki. She also came from a family rooted in the Christian faith, so we are equally yoked and on one accord with the gospel, as it pertains to how we should live and treat one another. We have found that marriage is the ultimate sacrifice of one's self and that godly love is the only thing that will keep you together. Four years later, our first child, Tiffani, was born, introducing us to the second stage of self-sacrifice and placed everything on a whole different level. Over the next ten years, the blessings continued to come through the birth of David II, Daniel, and Tia, four of the greatest kids in the universe. They all love the Lord, and just as my wife and I have done in the past, they try to serve God whenever they can with their time, talents, and resources. It was through this family relationship that I discovered nothing good is achieved without love and sacrifice. God so loved us that he sacrificed his only son Jesus Christ, who made the ultimate sacrifice for us with his life.

After the passing of my mother (Eleanor), from a short bout with cancer 1985, I was hearing the holy word every Sunday but not living it. I felt that my faith was broken and ineffective. While on a voluntary leave of absence from my airline job for three years in 2001 to pursue my dream of building homes, my father (Calvin) passed away suddenly in 2002 from natural causes. When you lose both parents early on in life, it can leave a void in your soul that I now realize; only God can fill. This is why I thank God for giving me a godly family and friends who will stand in the gap for me in my time of need.

Now, concerning my siblings, we were always active in my mother's family church. Our mom always had us in plays, choirs, and sometimes as ushers. As we grew older and moved out on our own, we continued to go to church and serve in various areas of the ministry. Renee, my older sister, served her church in Hampton, VA, and the Tidewater community until she became ill with a rare form of cancer in 2012 and passed one year later in the fall of in 2013. My younger brother Walter is a deacon, sound director, and bassist for the praise team at his church in Fredrick, MD. After he discovered Renee was ill, he started an e-mail ministry to help himself cope with the situation, which is outlined in his book "The Miracle of Transition." He continues this ministry and the e-mails have become a continual source of inspiration for all of his many followers includ-ing myself.

Early on in life, I discovered a deep passion for designing and building things out of wood and leather, assembling plastic models, auto repair, home improvement, as well as, listening and playing all forms of music. These hobbies have brought me great satisfaction and profits over the years, and I still indulge in them whenever I find the time. The Bible speaks to the purpose of God-given gifts and talents. He blesses us with them to bring pleasure to others and to ourselves. He even allows us to use them to make a living. Although writing has never been one of my passions, God used me to create this book so that you can discover how to take the faith that you have and make it healthier. Just like good eating habits strengthens the body, reading and studying God's word will strengthen our faith and boost our spiritual immune system, allowing us to cope with troubling situations that face us from time to time.

It is my sincere belief that *First Aid for the Spirit* was born out of my God-given creativity, with the sole purpose of helping you to strengthen and build up your faith to the degree that you will stand up to this sin sick world with renewed wisdom and godly insight as to who you really are and discover your true purpose and destiny. Remember, "In life great things are only achieved by way of love, faith and sacrifice."

In all things, be blessed.

CPSIA information can be obtained
at www.ICGtesting.com
Printed in the USA
LVHW041936150920
666053LV00006B/518